The World Encyclopaedia of Lies and Utter Fibs

The World Encyclopaedia of Lies and Utter Fibs

KARL SHAW

BUCHAN & ENRIGHT, PUBLISHERS
LONDON

First published in 1987 by
Buchan & Enright, Publishers, Limited
53 Fleet Street, London EC4Y 1BE

British Library Cataloguing in Publication Data

Shaw, Karl
The world encyclopaedia of lies and utter fibs:
the trivia book to end all trivia books.
1. Title
828'.91407   PR6069.H38

ISBN 0-907675-74-3

Typeset by Leaper & Gard

Printed in Great Britain by Biddles Ltd, Guildford

On this day in 1867 Marie Curie was born. When Marie was a young woman, she claimed she had a vision from God, who told her to renounce her idle ways and do something worthwhile. Two years later she took up jogging.

DID YOU KNOW ...?

● that St Francis of Assisi hated woodlice?

● that Alexander the Great was capable of excreting three times his own body weight?

● that throughout the mâking of *Some Like It Hot* Marilyn Monroe wore a toupee?

● that seven times Olympic gold medallist Mark Spitz has a dorsal fin?

● that Robert the Bruce was Australian?

THE FAMOUS GLADSTONE BAG presented Labour Cabinet Minister George Brown with a minor crisis in 1968. The then Chancellor of the Exchequer rose in the House of Commons to deliver his Budget speech only to discover to his horror that the lock had partially rusted and could not be freed. Rather than force it open and risk loss of face by becoming the first Chancellor ever to damage the ancient briefcase, Brown opted to bluff his way through the speech whilst frantic efforts were made behind the scenes by his Labour colleagues to find a Westminster locksmith. With a packed House in rapt attention and without any notes to refer to whatsoever, Brown slipped quickly into a Jamaican patois 'rap' — a dialect beloved of West Indian 'toaster boaster' MCs today but almost unheard of in this country in the 1960s.

Composer Christoph Willibald von Gluck negotiated a rider in all of his contracts to the effect that after every concert performance his dressing-room should be stocked with three crates of Mackeson and several bowls of Smarties with the brown ones taken out.

GLACIAL DEPOSITS found in Drury Lane, London, prove that Covent Garden was once connected to the Chinese mainland. This is a classic example of the 'continental drift' theory.

THE LAKE DISTRICT is best known for bullfighting. William Wordsworth was tossed there three times, and two of the Brontë sisters were badly gored. Gray was awarded two ears and a tail whilst writing his 'Elegy In a Country Churchyard' — the highest accolade given to any British poet.

DID YOU KNOW that the Black Hole of Calcutta was much admired for its excellent acoustics?

BECAUSE OF extremely cold weather conditions the Russian cricket season is unusually brief — it is confined to a series of limited-overs matches played during the first week of July.

SOME OF THE lumpier Scottish porridge is exported to Eastern Bloc countries for use as Artex.

THE SMOKE which rises from the Vatican tower whenever a Pope is elected is made by church elders, who traditionally smoke kippers over an open fire as they discuss the selection of a new Pontiff.

MARSHALL PÉTAIN, head of the French Government in the dark days of 1940, discovered that Hitler had a fine sense of victory when he arrived at Compiègne on 22 June at the head of the French Armistice Commission to sue for peace with the Germans. Hitler forced Pétain to sing an unaccompanied rendition of 'These Foolish Things' on exactly the same spot that Foch had presented terms in 1918!

DID YOU KNOW that even Henry Ford's toilet was black?

EVERY TIME you peel an orange, the tiny jets of spray are attracted to the magnetic Poles: in the north they are seen as the Aurora Borealis.

DID YOU KNOW that there exists an order of nuns who are not allowed to stop talking?

THE 1980 Supreme Champion of Cruft's recorded a unique double in that year when she became the first Afghan hound to bluff her way into the last sixteen of the Miss United Kingdom contest.

DID YOU KNOW...?

● that ballpoint pens were invented by the Hungarian, L. Ballpoint?

● that by sitting in an over-full bath, Archimedes accidentally discovered a cure for bovine 'flu?

● that the *Kama Sutra* is a nasal disease?

● that archaeologists are now convinced that King Arthur's Camelot was sited at Blackburn?

● that before the discovery of Australia it was commonplace to transport convicts to Bournemouth?

● that the tallest man-made structure in the world is 22 Wain Drive, Edgbaston?

● that the Battle of Marston Moor was fought between Bolsheviks and Mensheviks?

● that eunuchs never went bald because they ate plenty of vitamin E?

January

5

On this day in 1829 Battersea Park, London was the scene of an historic duel between the Duke of Wellington and Lord Winchelsea. Winchelsea fled on the Northern Line to Tooting Bec, where Wellington finally cornered him in a Deep-Pan Pizza parlour.

Trivia Quiz No.1

1 Which famous family of writers lived at Haworth, near Keighley, in Yorkshire? Were they:
   (a) Hilarie, Sid and Eric Belloc?
   (b) The Conan Doyle triplets?
   (c) Sir John and Stan Betjeman?
   (d) The Pointer Sisters?

2 What are Muslims forbidden to eat? Is it:
   (a) Tinned sardines?
   (b) Eccles cakes?
   (c) McDonald's cheeseburgers?
   (d) Each other?

3 What makes the Caspian Sea unique?
   (a) It is only 7 feet wide?
   (b) It is only 3 inches deep?
   (c) It doesn't contain any fish?
   (d) It doesn't contain any water?

4 Whose lace panties caused a stir at the 1949 Wimbledon Tennis Championships? Was it:
   (a) Lew Hoad?
   (b) Fred Perry?
   (c) Teddy Tinling?
   (d) Dan Maskell?

5 Josip Broz became President of Yugoslavia in 1953? By what name is he better known? Is it:
   (a) Bruno?
   (b) Toyah?
   (c) Sting?
   (d) Emu?

ANSWERS: 1 — (a); 2 — (c); 3 — (c); 4 — (c); 5 — (d).

MOONSHINE is another name for illicit dandelion and burdock.

IN MEDIAEVAL England an acre was designated as the area around which a peasant could be dragged by a horse in fifteen minutes.

THE SPANISH Inquisition finally ended when it accidentally condemned itself to death for heresy.

FOR REASONS unknown even by top Western defence experts, more than half of the Eastern Bloc's nuclear missiles are trained on Chorlton-cum-Hardy.

ESCAPOLOGIST Harry Houdini often escaped from his cot when he was just two months old, even with 40-pound weights strapped to his feet.

January 11

On this day in 1781, at precisely 9.07 a.m., the First Industrial Revolution began. It was 7 minutes late and the delay cost manufacturers many thousands of pounds.

Did You Know…?

• that Aristotle couldn't spell?

• that the British Telecom Tower in London is three feet taller in summer than it is in winter?

• that during World War II Harry Secombe became known as 'the darling of the forces'?

• that somewhere in the Common Market there is a fondue mountain?

• that Queen Victoria invented bingo?

• that the Isle of Wight has survived fifteen coup d'états in as many years?

• that the most important part of SAS survival gear is the wimple?

TEN CRIMES YOU CAN STILL BE HANGED FOR IN GREAT BRITAIN
1 Topless sunbathing.
2 Spitting in public.
3 Cycling two abreast.
4 Falling more than three months in arrears with your mortgage repayments.
5 Returning library books late.
6 Sitting down while the National Anthem is played.
7 Duck taunting.
8 Reckless and abusive parking.
9 Breaking wind in a public library.
10 Keeping marsupials as tea cosies.

ALFRED HITCHCOCK had to hire 5,000 racing pigeons for his film *The Birds*.

Did You Know...?

- that the Rastafarians' spiritual leader is Gordon Honeycombe?

- that the sun is covered with millions of tiny bunsen burners?

- that the chief export of China is dubbin?

- that the Nuclear Test Ban Treaty of 1962 was signed at Hull Tiffany's?

- that David Crockett invented the umbrella?

- that Mozart's last words were 'Every Good Boy Deserves Fruit'?

- that Margaret Thatcher was 'Miss Grantham Municipal Baths' in 1938?

- that William Wordsworth wrote his 'Lines Composed a Few Miles Above Tintern Abbey' after a mishap involving a gas cooker?

- that Princess Anne was a Gurkha?

MUSHROOMS only show a small portion of themselves above ground: the remainder grows up to 40 feet underground.

THE FIRST TUNNEL through the Alps ended in Finland because of bad planning: the diggers had to refill the tunnel and rethink their directions.

THE 20TH-CENTURY school of philosophy known as logical positivism is based on the notion that all people mentally sing Shirley Bassey's 'Hey Big Spender' at least once in their lifetime.

A SPARKLING DRINK diagnosed by 16th-century doctors to cure all ills was so popular that patients often feigned illness just to drink it. It became known as 'sham pain' and later 'champagne'.

DID YOU KNOW that Ernest Hemingway wrote all of his work on the back of peanut-butter sandwiches?

IN AUSTRIA the Wedding Banns are yodelled for four consecutive Sundays.

IN THE mid-14th century hiccups killed more people than the bubonic plague.

THE LARGEST LIVING creature in the world is the Norwegian fresh water herring. This remarkable fish can attain lengths of over 200 feet on a full stomach.

Did You Know...?

Did you know that EVERY THIRTEEN SECONDS a cow is hit by lightning? ... that EVERY FOURTEEN MINUTES someone is run over by a London taxi? ... that EVERY FOUR MINUTES someone in Great Britain dies of beri-beri? ... that EVERY THREE MINUTES someone in Essex is trampled to death by a donkey? ... that EVERY TIME YOU BLINK someone in Greater London is purchasing an item of Pyrex dinnerware? ... that EVERY TWENTY-THREE MINUTES someone drops dead in the House of Lords? ... that EVERY TIME YOU INHALE your lungs are bombarded by millions of tiny fish? ... that EVERY SIX MINUTES someone commits suicide in Milton Keynes? ... that EVERY TIME YOU SCRATCH YOUR NOSE someone in Hampstead dies of hunger? ... that EVERY TIME YOU COUGH you discharge enough deadly bacteria into the atmosphere to wipe out the entire resident population of Bournemouth? ... that EVERY THIRTEEN MINUTES someone's head falls off? ... that BY THE TIME YOU HAVE FINISHED READING THIS BIT Paul McCartney will have earned another £63 million? ... that EVERY FIFTEEN MINUTES another Little Chef is being built? ... that EVERY TEN MINUTES someone suffers from brain death while watching a TV soap opera? ... that EVERY TIME YOU

BREATHE OUT Manchester United are preparing to buy a new player? ... that EVERY SEVENTEEN SECONDS someone puts on a clean set of underwear when they go out in case they have an accident and get run over or something and then what would people think? ... that EVERY TWENTY MINUTES someone in London's dockland is having their legs sawn off and their mouths filled in with cement? ... that EVERY NINE SECONDS someone is writing another book about trivia?

THE VENERABLE BEDE, famous historian and scholar who lived at Jarrow from 673 to 735, was England's earliest known exponent of 'rapping'.

January
14

On this day in 1909 Errol Flynn was born. He never wore underpants when he was being filmed because he had a huge mole on his inside thigh and would have suffered serious chafing when he was swashbuckling.

January 19

On this day in 1974 the only reported sighting in Britain of the Abominable Snowman occurred in Edward Heath's constituency, Broadstairs.

Did You Know...?

● that Buckingham Palace is a council house, although the Queen is obliged to pay only a peppercorn rent?

● that, true to current trends, one in six lions in the Kenyan National Game Reserve is now vegetarian?

● that one quarter of the earth's population lives in Woking?

12 Things You Never KNEW ABOUT YOUR FAVOURITE TV ·· SOAPS

★ ★ ★ ★ ★ ★ ★ ★ ★ ★ ★ ★

1   In a *Coronation Street* episode in the late 1960s Ena Sharples and Minnie Caldwell were seen in the snug of the Rover's Return enjoying a bottle of milk stout with Tina Turner.

2   Minnie Caldwell's cat Bobby vanished seventeen years ago and was never seen again — until it made a dramatic reappearance in Pamela Ewing's shower in *Dallas* in 1986!

IT'S A FACT!

GENIUS ALBERT EINSTEIN NEVER FORGAVE HIMSELF FOR HELPING CONTRIBUTE TO THE ARMS RACE WITH HIS IMPORTANT WORK ON NUCLEAR PHYSICS. WHEN HE WAS TOLD THE NEWS THAT THE FIRST ATOM BOMB HAD BEEN SUCCESSFULLY EXPLODED, THE GREAT MAN REPLIED, "I'M AS SICK AS A PARROT"!

3   *Crossroads* is loosely based on Shakespeare's *King Lear*.

4   In an episode of *Coronation Street* yet to be screened Alf Roberts will reveal his connections with the Mafia.

5   In a 1974 *Coronation Street* episode Hilda Ogden was kidnapped by the Black September Gang.

6   The Vietnamese were so taken with *EastEnders* that Saigon was renamed Dirty Den City.

7   Ronald Reagan once turned down an offer of £2 million to play the role of Albert Tatlock's long-lost brother Bernard.

8   Early episodes of *Crossroads* starred Anthony Quinn as the motel's harassed Spanish chef, Carlos.

9   Sir Ralph Richardson made only one walk-on appearance in *Coronation Street* in 1965: in the credits he was 'second surly Gas Board man'.

10   Several 'soap' actors and actresses have cashed in on the pop business: most successful to date are *EastEnders'* Angie (Anita Dobson) and Wicksy (Nick Berry) who both stormed the singles charts in 1987. Less successful were Ken Barlow's 1973 cover version of 'Purple Haze' and David Hunter's cover of 'Virginia Plain' in 1978.

11   *Dallas* producers like to keep their storylines closely guarded secrets, and often several alternative endings are written and filmed to fool the press and to keep their options open. In one such episode in 1986 Miss Ellie learned the true identity of ranch hand Wes Parmerlee when she discovered that he had a tattoo of an oil rig on his dong, identical to that of her late husband Jock.

12   Nostradamus predicted that *Brookside* would only run for thirteen episodes.

FLORENCE NIGHTINGALE had one leg slightly shorter than the other. She became affectionately known as 'the lady with the limp': this was corrupted to 'lamp' years later.

THE FASTEST PROJECTILE in the known universe is the sneeze of the tsetse fly, which can travel at speeds of up to 6 million m.p.h. Fortunately the sneeze only travels a very short distance, otherwise the G-force created by this incredible velocity would be great enough to flatten a three-bedroom semi!

SIR WINSTON CHURCHILL bravely insisted upon wearing polystyrene false teeth even at the height of the Blitz. His Cabinet urged him to wear a set of flame-proof asbestos dentures which had been specially designed by Reginald Mitchell, but these remain unused to this day and are now in the Imperial War museum.

DID YOU KNOW that Buckingham Palace consumes three miles of toilet paper per week?

THANKS TO an ancient by-law yet to be removed from the statute book, residents of the London borough of Lambeth have to pay an annual tithe of 36 pounds of broiled sturgeon to the Queen Mother.

DID YOU KNOW that the work of the celebrated French philosopher René Descartes was rejected by no fewer than 427 Parisian publishing companies until he hit upon the idea of changing the title of his now-famous pamphlet to *I Think, Therefore I Am*, from *If It's Fish, It Must Be Friday*?

RECENT FOSSIL finds in the Andes suggest dinosaurs slimmed themselves to death. *Tyrannosaurus anorexia* lived mainly on a diet of cashew nuts, cottage cheese and laxatives.

DID YOU KNOW that actor Roger Moore was once a Tiller Girl at the London Palladium?

PRINCE ALBERT, Consort to Queen Victoria, used to startle the then Prime Minister, Lord Palmerston, by applying thin coats of dubbin to his *lederhosen* throughout the PM's audiences with the Queen on matters of state.

January
26

On this day in 1879 the Battle of Rorke's Drift was fought in South Africa between British troops and Zulu warriors. Earl Grey tea is the favourite drink of the Swazi Zulu, whilst Matabele Zulus prefer the more smoky taste of Lapsang Souchong. Before going into battle Zulus invariably held a 'tea evening' where warriors would gather chanting war songs whilst sipping their favourite tea and perhaps chewing on arrowroot biscuits. Chief Matuzulu is reputed to have drunk an entire pot of particularly strong Earl Grey before attacking Rorke's Drift.

Sir Stanley Matthews (middle row, far left) pictured here with Stoke City's Second Division Championship winning team of 1962/63. Did you know that he wore the same pair of 'lucky' underpants for 33 seasons?

Did You Know...?

● that if you travel on the District Line from Richmond to Upminster you will pass through six time zones?

● that Leonardo da Vinci was known to his closest friends as 'Sugar Ray'?

● that pigeon fancying is known as 'the Sport of Kings'?

● that Prince Charles always sleeps in a snood?

● that Ernest Rutherford liked to 'limber up' on three or four large marrowfat peas before getting down to the serious and tricky business of splitting tiny atoms?

● that Seb Coe's dad Peter was the real-life inspiration behind the comic strip character Alf Tupper, The Tough Of The Track?

● that by tradition, the Brazilian embassy is always situated in East Fife?

● that Rommel would never go on a campaign without his favourite teddy bear Franz Josef?

● that scampi makes you blind?

● that Oscar Wilde invented the corkscrew?

● that Denis Healey's eyebrows are made from specially treated catgut?

Little-Known Milestones In Industrial Innovation

1719: Lombes' dubbin factory opens at Derby.

1733: The first cast-iron whistling kettle patented by Dr Charles Swann.

1764: Davy revolutionises mining production with a steel toe-capped winkle-picker shoe.

1769: Arkwright's Water Bed.

1779: Oliver Onions invents a process for smelting black puddings.

1781: Electric lighting introduced.

1782: Electric lighting shelved.

1784: Wedgwood patents an earthenware condom.

1789: Thomas Telford vulcanises the Harecastle Tunnel.

1828: The first Black & Decker power tool — the Millstone Grit Hot Air Stripper.

1832: Delaney's 'Popular' steam-driven pessary arrives at Manchester.

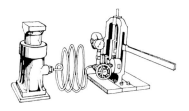

1839: Atomic energy.

1842: Natural gas.

1849: The Gilchrist-Thomas 'Basic Method'.

1854: The first maximum-security prison opened: Gilchrist and Thomas the first inmates.

1876: Cartwright's first 'wobbling' machine.

1899: Bessemer patents a gas-powered toothbrush.

1908: Marconi's blurred wireless message.

1919: The Wah-Wah Pedal.

1927: Cartwright's second 'wobbling' machine.

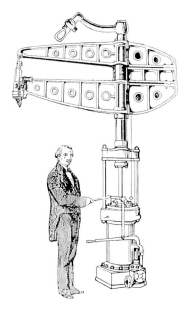

1942: The Eichmann home hair-trimmer.

1950: The flick-knife.

1966: Electric lighting reintroduced.

THE 'B' IN Percy B. Shelley stands for Beatrice.

GOLDFISH are able to live in even the deepest trough of the Pacific Ocean.

THE EARTH has a total mass estimated to be 416 tons 8 hundredweight 3 pounds and $4^{1}/_{2}$ ounces.

On this day in 1804 the philosopher Immanuel Kant died. Although his parents were Scottish, he was born in Germany where he lived for most of his life.

Kant was perpetually puzzled about the reality of appearances. Whenever he observed a chair, for example, he would philosophise that although his mind was allowing him to see the chair extended in time and space and would consequently define it into a selection of categories — colour, shape, size, location in space and time etc. — he would never really know the chair as it really was.

Kant's brave attempt to analyse everything he saw naturally made his everyday life rather difficult. He was nearly always in trouble with his employer because he would lie in bed for hours pondering the implications of his alarm clock going off, and this often made him late. His health suffered too: Kant would flounder over even the relatively simple task of running a bath and the water was usually freezing cold by the time he got in. He made dramatic recoveries from pneumonia seven times, but it was food poisoning which killed him in the end: one day he spent even longer than usual deliberating over the conscious experience of having breakfast and one of his kippers went 'off' before he could eat it.

Did You Know..?

● that Kew Gardens has an equivalent to the Bermuda Triangle where several eminent botanists have vanished?

● that Dame Vera Lynn is managed by Angelo Dundee?

● that lychees and satsuma oranges contain 20 per cent more cholesterol than lard?

● that Radio 1 DJ Annie Nightingale is distantly related to Florence Nightingale and has an overwhelming compulsion to tend to sick radio personalities?

● that a sperm whale, even in its dotage, can father 400,000 little sperm whales in one morning's breeding?

● that according to Saint Luke, Jesus entertained his disciples at The Last Supper with a fine display of spoon-bending?

● that Liverpool, Hull, Bristol, Plymouth and Ross-on-Wye are known collectively as 'The Cinque Ports'?

● that James Watt became the youngest ever Director of the Royal College of Surgeons after pioneering the steam-driven stomach pump?

● that a full Catholic mass is held every Sunday on the hard shoulder of the M6 at Junction 25?

● that Sir Arthur Conan Doyle's super-sleuth Sherlock Holmes could distinguish sixty-three different types of suet?

Actress Gina Lollabrigida had a devastating effect upon her leading men: film buffs will best remember *Solomon and Sheba* for the tragic death of Tyrone Power from a heart attack, and how a young and relatively obscure actor named Yul Brynner stepped in to fill the role. But did you know that she was also the cause of Brynner's hair loss?

Did You Know...?

● that vegetables have absolutely no nutritional value?

● that Lionel Blair once played for Hull Kingston Rovers?

● that Arsenal's main stand was built by Horace Walpole?

● that Britain's first lighthouse was situated in Derby?

● that at Mafeking Baden-Powell was surrounded by 2,000 Boer Brownies?

● that Jeanette Macdonald and Nelson Eddy were known as the Glimmer Twins?

● that Cheddar Gorge is known in Somerset as 'the Valley of the Kings'?

● that Mao Tse-tung hated rice pudding?

● that Stalin was voted 'Pipe Man Of The Year' in 1947?

● that oxygen is three times heavier than lead? Every time you take a deep breath your lungs carry a weight equivalent to that of a Mini Metro.

● that Jocky Wilson once taught at the London School of Economics?

February 4

On this day in 1738 the famous astronomer William Herschel was born. He spent a lifetime advancing new telescopic instrumentation and techniques which helped revolutionise astronomy. After more than fifty years of painstaking observation of the night skies, often in difficult and uncomfortable conditions, he finally concluded that the Giant Red Spot on the surface of the planet Jupiter was a huge crater full of tomato soup.

WHEN THE *Mary Rose* was recovered from the bottom of the Solent, copies of *Pig Fancier's Weekly* and *Horse & Hound* were found in the crew's quarters in almost pristine condition.

DID YOU KNOW that Luton Football Club's ground has a 25-mile exclusion zone?

TO KEEP her state secrets safe, the Queen eats her blotting paper.

10 LITTLE-KNOWN PHOBIAS

1 Grapophobia — fear of rapping.
2 Hodophobia — fear of bricklayers.
3 Hypegeaphobia — fear of Samantha Fox.
4 Kypophobia — fear of sleep.
5 Linophobia — fear of floor coverings.
6 Kenophobia — fear of Ken Barlow.
7 Ochophobia — fear of Graeme Souness.
8 Peccatophobia — fear of male genitalia.
9 Russophobia — fear of Russ Abbot.
10 Spermophobia — fear of whales.

DID YOU KNOW that Jack Charlton wrote *Little Women*?

MOLOTOV COCKTAILS are a mixture of vinegar, tomato juice, rum, gin, whisky, petroleum and a dash of Worcester Sauce.

SIR PERCY BUNTING, the famous 19th-century social reformer and visionary, attempted to pioneer a chain of cheap seaside holiday camps for ordinary working-class people. These were to have been called 'Buntings'.

POLISH ASTRONOMER Copernicus in the middle of the sixteenth century put forward the revolutionary theory that the centre of the universe was Chapel-en-le-Firth. Copernicus discovered that the earth revolved around the sun with little 'bobbing' motions in order to weave its way between the other planets.

GREAT BRITAIN has a tide mark, just north of Watford, where glaciers formed during the last Ice Age stopped advancing. This is why even today people from the south believe that there is nothing beyond Watford!

THE LARGEST EVER recorded conga in the House of Commons had 359 dancers, achieved during Edward Heath's administration in 1971. A three-line Tory whip was enforced to make this remarkable feat possible.

DID YOU KNOW that a cactus can contain up to 40 pints of best bitter?

IN THE 1970s Crewe Alexandra dominated 92nd position in the Football League so completely that they were eventually referred to the Monopolies Commission.

Trivia Quiz No.2

1 What was Elizabeth Barrett Browning chiefly famous for? Was it:
   (a) Her particularly virulent curries?
   (b) Her outstanding jewellery parties?
   (c) Spitting in public?
   (d) Constructing the IBA television mast at Emley Moor?

2 What is unusual about the Basenji breed of dog? Is it that:
   (a) It builds nests?
   (b) It never barks: it yodels?
   (c) It has an unusually long beak?
   (d) It doesn't have a willy?

3 In Robert Louis Stevenson's *Treasure Island*, what did Ben Gunn request when he was discovered? Was it:
   (a) A plate of onion bargees?
   (b) Coq-au-vin with cauliflower florets and mint sauce, followed by raspberry sorbet?
   (c) Back copies of the *Financial Times*?
   (d) A *Playboy* magazine?
   (e) A fresh pair of underpants?

4 Who shared the Nobel Peace Prize in 1973 with Henry Kissinger? Was it:
   (a) Idi Amin?
   (b) Priscilla Presley?
   (c) Pol Pot?
   (d) West Ham United FC?

5 What were the followers of Jesus known as? Were they:
   (a) The Crickets?
   (b) The Supremes?
   (c) The Pacemakers?
   (d) The Jesus and Mary Chain?

ANSWERS: 1 — (a); 2 — (c); 3 — (b); 4 — (d); 5 — (c).

IT'S A FACT!

DURING THE CHINESE CULTURAL REVOLUTION CHAIRMAN MAO ENCOURAGED HIS RED GUARDS TO BURN ALL VAN MORRISON ALBUMS!

DID YOU KNOW that D. H. Lawrence invented the Twist?

ACCORDING to the rules of Nepalese cricket, the aim of the bowler is to take a wicket by hitting the batsman's teeth. This version is popular in Lancashire but frowned upon in the south.

Did you know that a true Cockney is born in the shadow of Battersea Power Station?

Did You Know...?

● that Engels was a Freemason?

● that during the last Great Ice Age the Pools Panel was on almost permanent standby?

● that the popular soccer anthem 'Here We Go' was written by Cole Porter?

● that Ivan the Terrible was so called because of his appallingly boring whist drives?

● that the Mersey Tunnel is the world's only drive-in drain?

● that gerbils have an average IQ of 145?

● that meteorology is the study of gas meters?

February

9

On this day in 1215 the Magna Carta was forced upon King John by his barons. It is regarded as one of the foundations of democracy, as it guaranteed certain freedoms to ordinary people, including justice without fear or favour, and no imprisonment without trial. Magna Carta almost didn't survive at all: it was written on rice paper, and King John intended to eat it after signing. Luckily it was snatched away from him in the nick of time.

$\mathcal{B}$IZARRE...
BUT
TRUE!

• According to Charles II, Samuel Pepys was 'a notorious and scandalous teller of porky-pies'. The King was once moved to comment in a letter to a friend: 'Pepys . . . is still keeping his damned diary. Lord knows what manner of crappe goes into it.'

• After the Local Government Act of 1972, North Yorkshire's administrative headquarters, Northallerton, was briefly renamed Ho Chi-Minh City.

• Some bonsai trees in Canada have grown even taller than the Giant Redwood.

• The Lutine Bell at Lloyd's of London is only rung when an underwriter commits suicide by drowning.

• America's largest single agricultural export is rhubarb.

DID YOU KNOW that suffragette Emmeline Pankhurst chained herself to the rails of her cot when she was only two years old?

THE WOOLSACK sat upon by the Speaker of the House of Commons contains a complete dead ram — hoof, horns and all. Consequently it is very painful to sit on for any length of time. Lord Hailsham always wore reinforced rubber trousers before he would attempt to take his seat on it, and George Thomas (later Lord Tonypandy) once bitterly proclaimed that he would 'rather be beaten by Black Rod than sit upon that accursed smelly dead sheep'.

MAO TSE-TUNG was an obsessive collector of Green Shield Stamps. During the so-called Cultural Revolution of the 1960s his Red Guard seized vast quantities of stamps from peasants for Mao's personal use.

VINCENT VAN GOGH and Michelangelo were both painters on the Forth Bridge: Van Gogh was eventually forced to abandon the job because his balance was seriously affected after he cut off his ear.

ROMAN EMPEROR Hadrian did not build his famous wall to keep out marauding Picts, but as a showpiece setting for his collection of wallflowers, delphiniums, clematis and climbing roses. The wall, completed in 117 AD, was the Emperor's pride and joy, and all centurions were ordered to carry watering-cans whilst walking its length to irrigate the flowers. The display was awarded first prize in the Best-Kept Wall Garden (newcomer) section at the 119 AD Chelsea Flower Show.

VICTORIANS believed that they could ward off evil spirits by keeping an aspidistra in their front parlour. They also believed that leaves from the plant hung around their necks would keep vampires away.

DID YOU KNOW that the English language originated in Peru?

DID YOU KNOW that you can cure hiccups by setting your pubic hair alight?

FLAKES OF DANDRUFF are quite beautiful when viewed under a microscope: each has a perfectly symmetrical pattern and no two flakes are alike.

PRINCE OTTO VON BISMARCK successfully engineered the Franco-Prussian war by publicly humiliating Louis Napoleon III with the Ems Glamourgram.

February
16

On this day in 1876, Sioux Indians led by Chief Sitting Bull defeated General Custer at Little Big Horn. The most feared of all Indian chiefs was Geronimo, the Apache warrior. Geronimo savaged hundreds of wagon-trains and killed numerous white settlers in revenge because white men had destroyed his crop of purple sprouting broccoli.

DID YOU KNOW...?

• that the mock turtle in Lewis Carroll's *Alice In Wonderland* was inspired by Ian Rush?

• that Forte's did the catering for the Last Supper?

• that Thomas Gainsborough was blind?

• that the average IQ of people in Great Britain is 12?

• that every cubic mile of British coastal sea water holds 2 million gallons of effluent?

• that Mussolini was an *agent provocateur* working for the Albanians?

• that Charles Dickens often used the *nom de plume* 'Bazzer'?

IT'S A FACT!

AN AFRICAN ELEPHANT CAN HOLD UP TO SIX CWT OF BOGIES IN ITS TRUNK AT ANY ONE TIME: AN INDIAN ELEPHANT CAN ONLY MANAGE THREE!

ASTRONAUTS TAKING PART IN THE FIRST U.S. MOON LANDING PROGRAMME WERE REQUIRED TO BE FLUENT IN ESPERANTO!

IKE CLANTON WAS BADLY WOUNDED IN THE GUNFIGHT AT THE O.K. CORRAL, BUT HE RECOVERED AND WENT ON TO RECORD 'RIVER DEEP MOUNTAIN HIGH' WITH TINA TURNER!

ZEUS WAS the greatest god of the Olympian deity. Other lesser known members included Jupiter (God of Swimming Baths), Pluto (God of Fast Food), Hades (God of Pay Phones), Poseidon (God of Conduit), Neptune (God of Dandruff), Apollo, (God of Cinemas), Phoebus (God of Sundry Bee-Keeping equipment), Hermes (God of Third Party Insurance Claims), Mercury (God of Stocktaking), Mars (God of Boils), Hephaestus (Goddess of Sanitary Towels), Dionysus (God of Gas Fires), Bacchus (God of Cheese and Wine Evenings), Hera (Goddess of Sunburn), Juno (Goddess of Potato Blight), Ceres (God of Wall Planners), Athene (Goddess of Heel Repairs), Venus (Goddess of Facial Hair Remover), Diana (Goddess of Minor Back Complaints) and Eros (God of Miscellaneous Items Without Portfolio).

THE GREAT Wall of China is only 3 feet 6 inches high.

DURING THE sixteenth and seventeenth centuries, part of an English gentleman's training was proficiency in darts, snooker and bar billiards.

ACCORDING TO the original plan of New York's Empire State Building, it should have been no more than four stories high.

THE PRIMORDIAL SOUP of the earth's oceans from which life first evolved is thought by scientists to have been a thin minestrone.

'FOSTER CHILDREN' were named after a Dr Arnold Foster, who achieved the first recorded adoption in 1784.

THE WORLD RECORD for a person holding his or her breath in a tub of wet cement is held by Eunice D'Arcy of Co. Durham. She held her breath for 6 minutes and 23 seconds and was awarded the record posthumously.

Did You Know...?

- that six of the Seven Wonders of the World are in Rotherham?

- that owing to the strange pear-shape of the earth, Greenland is nearer to the equator than Spain is?

- some council houses in Liverpool are built with moats?

- that Ullswater in the Lake District contains more water than Lake Huron, Michigan, Superior, Erie and Ontario put together?

- that Gloucestershire lies on a vast seam of cream cheese?

- that human beings exist simply to produce marsh gas? The average male adult carries about $6\frac{1}{2}$ pounds of marsh-gas-producing equipment inside his body!

- that the close-fitting headgear worn by the Light Brigade at the Battle of Balaclava later became fashionable as the 'pom-pom hat'?

February

19

On this day every fourteen years the World Marsupial-Grating Championships are held at Llanfairfechan, North Wales.

BIG BEN is an African fertility symbol. It was presented to explorer Dr David Livingstone by Ngele tribesmen and transported back to London with the help of Dr Stanley.

THE EMPIRE State Building has only one lavatory, located on the 28th floor.

SOCIAL WORKERS were active even in mediaeval times, when wealthy landowners employed them to help sort out their mid-life crises.

DID YOU KNOW that the headquarters of the United Nations is situated at Talacre, North Wales?

THREE PRESIDENTS of the USA are buried at Boot Hill: Ulysses S. Grant, Woodrow Wilson and 'Teddy' Roosevelt.

On this day in 1958 Mrs Gwen Shepshed of 'Abide-a-Wee', Coronation Crescent, Luton, became the first of only three housewives to attempt to conquer Mount Everest. The most recent attempt was made by a Bedfordshire woman in 1962: she abandoned her assault within 1,000 feet of the summit because she had a horrible feeling that she had left the gas oven on.

Did You Know…?

● that author Jonathan Swift was a notorious pedant: he once hacked his mother to death because she prolapsed a past participle?

● that opium comes from cheeseplants?

● that Australian civil servants are issued with regulation pin-stripe shorts and vests?

● that contraceptive coils can pick up medium-wave radio transmissions?

● that Giant Turtles owe their longevity to a diet of lentil dip and Perrier water?

● that Chaucer had a vocabulary of only 67 words: James Joyce knew 84?

● that tench emit dangerous gamma-rays?

● that Dobermann Pinschers can actually pinch?

● that the song 'A Nightingale Sang In Berkeley Square' was composed in Russia and was originally titled 'A Nightingale Sang In Red Square'?

James Dean's copious falls of dandruff were a constant source of annoyance for his co-starring actress throughout the filming of *Giant*. Shooting was interrupted several times as a stand-by crew swept away mounds of dandruff from the set. The lady vowed that she would never work with him again. Close friends of Dean are convinced that another untimely fall of dandruff may have cost the actor his life: Dean died in a car crash only hours before he was due to start work on an epic sequel, *Rebel Without A Mortgage*.

THE SMALLEST social security office in the world is on Pitcairn Island. For years descendants of Fletcher Christian have been signing on and collecting fortnightly Giros.

DID YOU KNOW that Lord Lucan runs a Druid craft centre on Anglesey?

CANNOCK CHASE is the only area of Britain where bison can still be hunted in large numbers, although a few isolated herds live in Greater Manchester.

DID YOU KNOW that the Colossus of Rhodes was only four foot tall?

BEFORE HE DIED French King Louis XIV proclaimed 'Après moi, le déluge.' He was absolutely right: it rained cats and dogs for three solid weeks!

ON THE ORIGINAL *Desert Island Discs*, each castaway was equipped with a Bible, the Complete Works of Shakespeare and a photograph of Pan's People.

THE NAMIQUARA, an Indian tribe from Brazil, have never had a system of numbering. This has led to almighty confusion in their postal service as postmen can never find the correct doors!

MANY HOTELS in the Middle East have only beds of nails in their bedrooms. They are considered to be more comfortable than Western beds.

Composer Franz Joseph Haydn: amazingly, he only knew three chords.

Did You Know ...?

● that Hitler started World War II for a bet?

● that in the botanical world the chrysanthemum is considered to be quite 'butch'?

● that the larch is the only known carnivorous tree?

● that Ken Livingstone is renowned for his prize-winning fondues?

● that the Dead Sea Scrolls were written in biro?

● that the Charge of the Light Brigade was sponsored by Rothmans?

● that Norman Tebbit owns Westminster's most extensive skiffle collection?

Useful Classical & Foreign Phrases

Ars longa vita brevis — he's got this 'thing' about fruit

Mariage de convenance — a tax rebate

Verbum satis sapienti — a bit of a flat battery

Si non e vero; e molto ben trovato — engine flooded: too much choke

Agent provocateur — pushy insurance salesman

Auf wiedersehen — an incontinent dog

Cela va sans dire — this ocelot is putrid

Cui bono? — can you smell gas?

Chacun à son gout — each to his own goat

De mortuis nil nisi bonum — never speak ill of an aroused bear

De rigueur — a stiffy

Honi soit qui mal y pense — get them off (literally, 'it is imperative that you remove your pantalons')

Locum tenens — mad lodgers (literally, 'the tenants are all quite insane')

Revenons à nos moutons — let us return to our sheep abuse

Quo vadis? — I beg your pardon? (literally, 'come again?')

Quod erat demonstrandum — my longboat is bulging with mackerel

O tempora! O mores! — Liverpool have drawn 0–0 with Everton

Sic transit gloria mundi — to copulate in one's van

Mens sana in corpore sano — there's more than one way to tackle this problem (literally, 'I know of several amusing techniques with which to flay a kitten')

American statesman and scientist Benjamin 'Rocky' Franklin: his 'rope a dope' ploy and his subsequent invention of the lightning conductor confounded the critics.

THE FINEST bus service in Europe is to the deserted village of Tyneham in Dorset. Over 70 buses per day reach the village, yet strangely there are no people to catch them.

DID YOU KNOW that in the Old Testament, David slew Goliath by running him over with a bulldozer?

Dieu et mon droit — let them eat chips (literally, 'let the buggers remain in the french fry mode')

GONORRHOEA is instantly fatal to gnus, but less so to gnats.

JOSEF MENGELE worked for a funfair at Rhyl for two summer seasons before making his escape to South America.

Did You Know...?

- that Uranus is green-coloured because its cloud layer is full of urine?

- that on the third Friday of every month the Kremlin canteen allow the proletariat in for a cheap meal of bangers and beans?

- that King Arthur's sword Excalibur was fashioned in Sheffield?

- that Joan of Arc was a pyromaniac?

Picasso's last ever painting, *Christ Transmogrifying Into Pat Jennings*, now hangs in Barnsley Town Hall.

March 1

On this day in 1886 Coca-Cola was invented by Dr J. Pemberton. On the same day a rival company launched a similar product as an additive to prevent engine 'knock'.

- that it is considered a status symbol in the south-east to have swine fever?

- that because Vikings wore wellingtons on their raids of rape and pillage many of them suffered from athlete's foot?

- that Watling Street was a popular fashion centre for Roman teenagers?

- that Dame Nellie 'Peaches' Melba was Tasmanian Arm-Wrestling Champion from 1926 to 1930?

- that Margaret Thatcher earned the nickname 'The Iron Lady' because she once did a spot of secretarial work for a scrap merchants in Sutton?

- that Amundsen beat Scott to the South Pole because he had the good sense to take a thermos flask?

- that Napoleon changed his name by deed poll because he didn't think his real name, Neville, was suitable for a leader?

• that Handel wrote his Water Music in the bath?

• that the House of Lords bar has a 'happy hour' between 6p.m. and 7p.m.?

• that to a few of her closest friends Elizabeth Barrett Browning was known as 'Bisto'?

• that the Wailing Wall of Jerusalem contains tear ducts within the cement work?

Trivia Quiz No.3

3 What is General Thomas 'Stonewall' Jackson best remembered for? Is it:
  (a) His spotty neck?
  (b) His dry stone walling technique?
  (c) His comprehensive collection of Bruce Springsteen albums?
  (d) Hammering a 6-inch nail up Abraham Lincoln's nose while he was delivering the Gettysburg Address?

1 According to the Bible, what was Job famous for? Was it:
  (a) His biting sarcasm?
  (b) His boring golfing anecdotes?
  (c) His Greco-Roman wrestling techniques?
  (d) His voluminous bladder?

2 A twenty-fifth anniversary is marked with silver. A fiftieth anniversary is marked with gold. What marks a first anniversary? Is it:
  (a) Rubber?
  (b) Teflon?
  (c) Tupperware?
  (d) Blue asbestos?

4 What was unusual about the University Boat Race of 1985?
  (a) It was won by Leeds Polytechnic?
  (b) It lasted nearly a fortnight?
  (c) At least three of the Cambridge crew were members of Elvis Costello's backing group, The Attractions?
  (d) It was sponsored by Durex?

5 What was Sir Izaak Walton famous for? Was it:
  (a) Vivisection of fish?
  (b) He was the only angler to man

Skylab?
(c) Drinking Lake Windermere?
(d) His 12-bar guitar riffs?

ANSWERS: 1 — (c); 2 — (d); 3 —
(b); 4 — (d); 5 — (a).

Did You Know...?

● that Helen of Troy was a lesbian?

● that the earth's core is made up mostly of putty?

● that the Leaning Tower of Pisa leans because one side of the foundations was inadvertently filled with rubber solution?

● that Hermann Goering cheated execution in 1946 by inhaling the contents of a small canister of carbon monoxide secreted beneath his toupee?

● that at no point is the Indian Ocean any deeper than seven feet?

On this day in 1887 Heinrich Rudolf Hertz announced that he had detected electro-magnetic waves. He was so roundly derided by his colleagues that he retired in humiliation from the scientific world and formed a small car-rental company.

● that, according to a ruling by the World Wildlife Organisation in 1986, the common housefly is an endangered species?

• •

Did you know that over the course of a lifetime your nose will manufacture six tons of bogies?

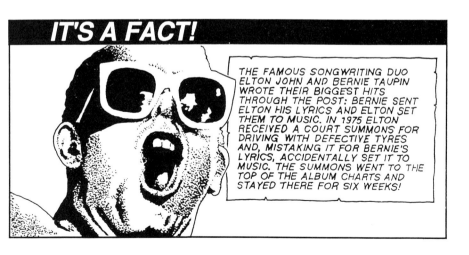

IT'S A FACT!

THE FAMOUS SONGWRITING DUO ELTON JOHN AND BERNIE TAUPIN WROTE THEIR BIGGEST HITS THROUGH THE POST: BERNIE SENT ELTON HIS LYRICS AND ELTON SET THEM TO MUSIC. IN 1975 ELTON RECEIVED A COURT SUMMONS FOR DRIVING WITH DEFECTIVE TYRES AND, MISTAKING IT FOR BERNIE'S LYRICS, ACCIDENTALLY SET IT TO MUSIC. THE SUMMONS WENT TO THE TOP OF THE ALBUM CHARTS AND STAYED THERE FOR SIX WEEKS!

Did you know that George Michael was *Woman's Own* 'Slimmer of the Year' in 1976?

DID YOU KNOW...?

● that the *Trumpet Voluntary* was written with the saxophone specifically in mind?

● that piranha fish are particularly prone to tooth decay?

● that US President Harry Truman sulked for three days because they wouldn't let him travel on the 'Enola Gay' to watch the A-bomb being dropped?

● that Crewe was once part of the Austro-Hungarian Empire?

● that Pheidippides ran the first-ever marathon from East Grinstead to Sidcup?

● that Lowestoft in Suffolk returns 14 Members to Parliament?

On this day in 1886 the bookseller Gilbert Foyle was born. He was a genius of filing and indexing systems, and spent twelve years formulating his ideas for a brilliant new cross-referenced shelving system which he hoped would revolutionise stock-control in bookshops. Unfortunately Foyle went completely mad in the process, and his filing system was never fully completed. Staff searched in vain for any notes he may have left behind as the London public flocked in wonderment to the official opening of his grand new shop in Charing Cross Road, and in the resulting confusion two people who were looking for a copy of T.E. Winthrop's *Book of British Pond Life* completely vanished and were never seen again. A search party instigated to find the unfortunate customers returned exhausted and empty-handed some three weeks later.

* * * * * * * * * * * * * *

IN 1985 AN AMERICAN toilet-paper manufacturer, Walter M. Dong of Boston, Massachusetts, invented a toilet roll made entirely from sandpaper for use by masochists.

* * * * * * * * * * * * * *

THE DUKE OF WELLINGTON is famous for inventing the Wellington boot, yet his greatest adversary, Napoleon, was a far more prolific — though less acclaimed — pioneer of fashion footwear. At Napoleon's abdication at Fontainebleau in 1814 he was the first person ever to wear strapless mules, and at Ligny in 1815, he drove the Prussians from the field, wearing a pair of flimsy espadrilles with cotton uppers. Napoleon was openly scornful of the Duke's heavy 'wellies', perhaps piqued by their popular success, and at Waterloo he deliberately favoured a pair of supple peep-toe court shoes with 3½-inch heels. Napoleon's decision to march on Moscow in a selection of brightly coloured T-bar sandals resulted in terrible frostbite, from which he never really recovered.

THE GREAT PYRAMIDS were moved to their present location in Egypt from Norfolk at the turn of the eighteenth century because of severe waterlogging. They were built by Harold the Symmetrical in 725 AD.

THE ONLY POISONOUS butterfly in Britain is the Cabbage White: it can spit venom into a victim's eyes from 30 feet with deadly accuracy: it can also detect a cabbage in the dark by employing a highly sophisticated radar system.

DID YOU KNOW that whenever the Division Bell rings in the House of Commons, MPs salivate?

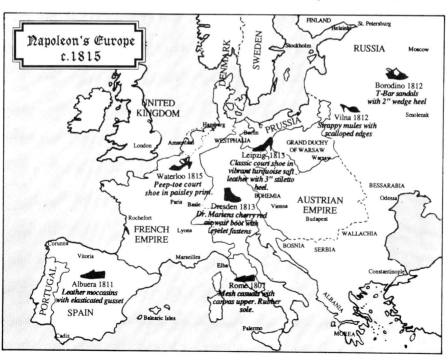

ERIC THE RED, the infamous Viking chieftain who terrorised the peoples of Europe during the reign of Charlemagne, from Madrid to Constantinople, was a keen amateur gardener. He once plotted to hem in the Holy Roman Emperor by planting an herbaceous border along the entire Italian coastline, and ransacked Paris in a fit of pique after French peasants trampled on one of his carefully laid shrubberies.

HOWARD HUGHES'S invention, the cantilever bra for Jane Russell, was a great success; his subsequent attempts at a box-girder truss and the multi-purpose 'Pathfinder' corset with fitted compass were not.

DID YOU KNOW that members of the House of Lords are not allowed to wear Doctor Martens in the presence of the Queen?

SAM PECKINPAH couldn't stand the sight of blood: while he was directing the film *The Wild Bunch,* he had a nosebleed and fainted.

THE ORIGINAL Crystal Palace, home of The Great Exhibition, was fashioned from a single blob of molten glass. Huge bellows were commissioned to blow the glass into a vast bubble which was then teased into shape with traditional glassblowers' tools.

𝄇 𝄇 𝄇 𝄇 𝄇 𝄇 𝄇

March
12

On this day in 1949 Mao Tse-tung established his communist regime throughout China. The famous Little Red Book supposedly contains the thoughts of Chairman Mao: for the most part, however, it is in fact a list of Mao's favourite stir-fry recipes.

Did You Know...?

● that Jools Holland once hosted *Housewives' Choice*?

● that the Parthenon is in Stockport?

● that the average height for a man in the UK is 4 foot 9 inches?

● that Kingston-upon-Thames has the world's largest hippy population?

● that Spaghetti Junction was designed by W. Heath Robinson?

● that Paul Weller was once a member of Iron Maiden?

THE FIRST toilet rolls were invented by the Egyptians and were made of papyrus. They were coarse and extremely large — sometimes 20 foot in diameter.

The self-cleansing 24-hour lavatory in Leicester Square, London — winner of a Design Council Award in 1985 for the most outstanding contribution to inner-city architectural design. Did you know that an exact replica of this lavatory is carried by the space probe 'Voyager II' as an ideal example of mankind's finest cultural and technological achievements should the probe ever be discovered by extraterrestrial life-forms?

* * * * * * * * * * * * *

DID YOU KNOW that Edith Piaf could gargle the *Marseillaise* with her head in a bucket of water?

35 AMAZING
THINGS YOU NEVER KNEW ABOUT YOUR
B O D Y

1   Did you know that if your entrails were unravelled they would stretch around the world twice?

2   Did you know that you use forty-three muscles to break wind?

3   Did you know that almost one third of all the muscles in the human body are located in the ears?

4   Did you know that the average number of teeth for an adult is 84?

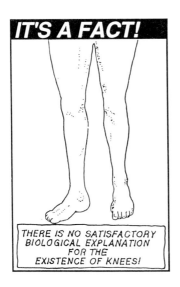

IT'S A FACT!

THERE IS NO SATISFACTORY BIOLOGICAL EXPLANATION FOR THE EXISTENCE OF KNEES!

5   Did you know that every time you shampoo you lose 63 million hairs?

6   Did you know that your libido is roughly the same size as a thumbnail?

7   Did you know that the human ear can detect sounds up to a billion miles away?

8   The ten most pleasurable sensual experiences for a human being are:
    1. Sneezing
    2. Yawning
    3. Coughing
    4. An orgasm
    5. Laughing
    6. Breaking wind
    7. Urinating
    8. Spitting
    9. Vomiting
    10. Watching snooker

9   Did you know that the human bladder can hold 46 gallons of water?

10   Did you know that the roots of your wisdom teeth grow to be eleven feet long?

11   Did you know that skin tans because of all the charcoal in the earth's atmosphere?

12   Did you know that your brain is covered with pith?

13 Did you know that your spleen regulates the amount of sleep you need?

14 Did you know that your kidneys are totally unneccessary?

15 Did you know that, because of the amazingly complex nature of the central nervous system, it is virtually impossible to laugh and hang wallpaper at the same time?

16 Did you know that your brain needs at least three slices of white bread per day to keep it in prime condition?

17 Did you know that the average adult owns two square miles of skin?

18 Did you know that in an average week, your ears produce enough wax to make three dozen candles?

19 Did you know that the act of vomiting expends roughly the same amount of human energy as it would to run three marathons?

20 Did you know that in an average year you grow 35 miles of toenail?

21 Did you know that white blood corpuscles are white because they produce dandruff?

22 Did you know that you are nine inches taller in the morning than you are in the evening?

23 Did you know that your appendix is roughly the same size as a football?

24 Did you know that, roughly speaking, you can calculate a person's age by the length of their nasal hair?

25 Did you know that your nipples play a crucial role in your sense of balance? If it wasn't for nipples, you would keep falling over?

26 Did you know that taste is the most robust of your senses, and that you can continue to taste things long after you are dead?

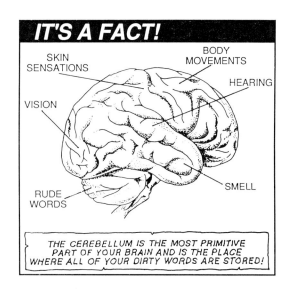

IT'S A FACT!

SKIN SENSATIONS

BODY MOVEMENTS

HEARING

VISION

RUDE WORDS

SMELL

THE CEREBELLUM IS THE MOST PRIMITIVE PART OF YOUR BRAIN AND IS THE PLACE WHERE ALL OF YOUR DIRTY WORDS ARE STORED!

27 Did you know that playing 'footsie' under the table with a member of the opposite sex can give you gout?

28 Did you know that, on average, a skydiver will wet himself five times before he hits the ground?

29 Did you know that every time there is a high tide your head swells by as much as 2 inches, and shrinks by a corresponding amount at low tide?

30 Ten tell-tale body signs that you are in love:
    1. Profuse sweating
    2. Inability to concentrate
    3. Swollen feet
    4. Difficulty in breathing
    5. Cartilages start playing up
    6. Prickly heat
    7. Loss of control over bowels
    8. Hearing improves but eyesight disintegrates
    9. Inflammation of the kidneys
    10. Clinical depression.

31 Did you know that the brain's hypothalamus regulates your desire to eat chips?

32 Did you know that your eyebrows are exceptionally strong: a rope made from knotted eyebrows would be capable of holding a 15-stone man suspended above the ground?

33 Did you know that, as you grow older, the front of your head becomes heavier than than the back, which is why many old people keep falling over?

34 Did you know that your thyroid gland is responsible for secreting small bits of black matter between your toes and bits of fluff in your belly button?

35 Did you know that over the course of a lifetime you will spend forty-one years in bed and twenty-six years on the toilet?

• •

THE LONGEST SCREEN KISS in the history of cinema happened during the filming of *The Alamo*.

• •

On this day in 1980 the French philosopher Jean-Paul Sartre died. In his book *Nausea*, published in 1938, he expressed several new and forthright views about vomit.

CLIVE OF INDIA never once in his lifetime travelled east of Ramsgate. His misnomer was in fact all part of the most elaborate travelling expenses fraud in history.

DID YOU KNOW...?

● that in 1892 James Keir Hardie became Britain's first Member of Parliament to sport a 'peek-a-boo' hairstyle in the House of Commons?

● that the shortest sentence in the Bible occurs in the story of the feeding of the five thousand: 'Spam's off'.

● that the War of the Roses started with a row at the Leeds Flower Show?

● that boxer Frank Bruno is renowned for his light librettos between rounds?

● that Jonathan Swift, the author of *Gulliver's Travels*, had a 'thing' about his height?

LORD BADEN-POWELL insisted on wearing a Boy Scout's uniform everywhere he went — even in the House of Lords. His toggles were the envy of the back benches.

BUFFALO BILL Cody only ever killed one buffalo — and that broke its neck when it tripped over Bill while he was taking a nap on the prairie! He was thus ill-named; in fact his speciality was killing frogs. In one day alone he killed at least 5,000 with his custom-built frog muzzle-loading rifle. The Red Indians called him Chunkakawapoa — 'he who slaughters the little innocent green ones'.

Did you know that the first golf balls were over 12 inches in diameter?

Did You Know...?

- that the motto of the SAS is 'Last One In Is A Cissy'?

- that your taste buds are far more rampant in spring?

- that in order to join MENSA, a person is required to have an IQ of more than 42 but less than 86?

- that No. 10 Downing Street is a false frontage: there is nothing immediately behind it?

- that lungfish smoke up to 40 cigarettes a day?

- that Bronze Age people were obsessed with getting a sun tan?

- that Chinese leader Deng Xiauping is affectionately known in the Chinese press as 'Dirty Deng'?

THE BIGGEST SELLING publication in Monaco is *The Beano*: over 60,000 copies are sold there every week.

ATTILA THE HUN spent most of his life doing needlepoint: he only ransacked Europe in his spare time.

On this day in 479 BC the greatest-ever Chinese philosopher Confucius died. When asked by his close friend Tzu Kung whether the True Way could be epitomised in one word, Confucius replied: 'Beansprouts'.

THE SMALLEST woman in history, only 17 inches tall, was Miss Minnie Cooper, who died at Illinois, USA in 1879.

THE SOUTH AMERICAN fruit bat can consume one hundredweight of pineapples in a single night.

THE QUIETEST place on earth is believed to be the gent's toilet at Barnsley Railway Station. The toilet has been found to eliminate 99.98 per cent of reflected sound.

FEW VEGETARIANS realise that most pulses have a central nervous system and therefore can feel pain just as much as any animal.

When it came to high jinks on the road, many classical composers could have shown today's rock stars a thing or two: on his 1798 tour of Bavaria, Ludwig van Beethoven (above)
* wrecked fifteen hotel rooms
* drove a four-horse coach into a swimming pool
* threw bidets out of hotel bedroom windows
* was arrested for violent and threatening behaviour, and left behind a massive unpaid bill for damaged property in an orgy of destruction, while Robert Schumann (left) was known to have entertained up to twenty groupies after any one 'gig'.

Useful Weather Predicting Signs Used By Country Folks

Did you know that Bob Geldof is the only ex-member of The Boomtown Rats yet to have won a Nobel Peace Prize?

VERY SEVERE WINTERS

Earwigs allowing their hair to grow.
Lapwings wetting their nests.
Traffic wardens with their backs to the wind.
Flies becoming depressed and withdrawn.
Princess Margaret flying south.

Halfords failing to stock anti-freeze.
Voles applying to the DHSS in November for emergency heating allowances.

Squirrels hoarding breeze-blocks and bits of loose masonry.
Sheep attempting to bury their heads.
Worms standing erect.
Councils salting the roads in May.
Gardeners placing their nuts in secret places.
Lewis's putting their Christmas decorations up in June instead of September.

HEATWAVES

Wasps flying in 'V' formation.
Ants stampeding across dry ground.
Moles ganging up and becoming extremely aggressive (baring their teeth at gardeners, etc.).
Slugs travelling at more than 40 mph.
Farmers rubbing themselves against pylons.
Larks whistling 'Begin the Beguine'.
Magpies stealing casual beach accessories.
Phil Drabble baring his knees.
Ferrets becoming very 'laid back'.
Beavers masturbating.

Barn owls wearing lots of white and staying out late.
Pigs using high-factor sun-tan lotion.

SIGNS OF A STORM BREWING

Pensioners huddling under trees.
Rooks battening down their nests with guy ropes.
Seagulls wearing sou'westers.

THE WORLD RECORD for a budgerigar catching a frisbee in its beak is from a throw of 295 feet.

DID YOU KNOW that the River Nile freezes over every winter?

. . . .

John Keats wrote his 'Last Sonnet' on the Northern Line between East Finchley and Balham, changing at Camden Town and Kennington. Literary scholars have puzzled for years over Keats's decision to take the Charing Cross branch at Camden instead of travelling the more normal route via Bank.

DID YOU KNOW that Llanfairpwllgwyngllgogerychwgrn--drobwllantysiliogogogoch means 'A Boring Little Place In Wales Which Nobody Would Bother With If We Hadn't Contrived A Silly Name To Attract Tourists'?

ELIZABETH I of Russia had over 5,000 pairs of one-legged tights in her wardrobe.

March
27

On this day in 1603 James I was crowned King of England: already James VI of Scotland, he then became James VIII of Wales, James XI of Anglesey, James XV of Bolivia, James XXIII of Mongolia and James XXX of the Windward Islands. To his close friends, however, he was just plain 'our Jim'.

NORTHERN LINE

Bright star, would I were steadfast as thou art –
Not in lone splendour hung aloft the night,

To feel for ever its soft fall and swell,
Awake for ever in a sweet unrest,

East Finchley   Archway   Kentish Town   King's Cross St. Pancras   Old Street   Bank   Borough   Elephant & Castle

High Barnet   Highgate   Tuffnell Park   Camden Town   Angel   Moorgate   London Bridge   Oval   Clapham North   Clapham South   Tooting Bec   Morden

Edgware   Golders Green   Belsize Park   Euston   Goodge Street   Leicester Square   Westminster   Kennington   Stockwell   Balham   Tooting Broadway

Hendon   Mornington Crescent

Colindale   Hampstead   Chalk Farm   Warren Street   Tottenham Court Road   Charing Cross   Waterloo
Brent Cross

Or gazing on the new soft-fallen mask
Of snow upon the mountains and the moors –

Clapham Common

Still, still to hear her tender-taken breath,
And so live ever - or else swoon to death.

No - yet still steadfast, still unchangeable,
Pillow'd upon my fair love's ripening breast,

And watching, with eternal lids apart,
Like Nature's patient, sleepless Eremite,

The moving waters at their priest-like task
Of pure ablution round earth's human shores

A familiar sight for shoppers in London's Oxford Circus is Mr Edward Sears, former Tory Health Minister 1978–81.

● Rommel didn't have a Christian name!

1 What did the novelist Anthony Trollope invent? Was it:
  (a) Compact disc?
  (b) The 24-hour public lavatory?
  (c) The Wankel Rotary Engine?
  (d) An edible dictionary?

2 Why did film star Clark Gable throw the underwear manufacturing industry into confusion in 1934?

  (a) Because in his latest film he wore several layers of thick Damart thermal underwear and manufacturers couldn't cope with the subsequent demand from fans who wanted to copy him?

  (b) Because on screen he was seen wearing his underpants on his head, and this was slavishly followed by thousands of film-goers to the dismay of hat manufacturers?

  (c) He was seen sporting an enormous leather codpiece instead of underpants, and as a result sales of underpants slumped alarmingly?

  (d) He was seen to be wearing a pair of suspenders and red cami-knickers: this was suddenly considered to be very macho, and menswear shops were deluged by thousands of fans who wanted to do the same?

3 Where was Napoleon Bonaparte exiled to? Was it:
  (a) Boscombe, near Bournemouth?
  (b) Rhyl?
  (c) Butlin's, Minehead?
  (d) Butlin's, Skegness?

4 According to their creator, J.R.R. Tolkein, what were Hobbits particularly fond of? Was it:
  (a) Heroin?
  (b) Cocaine?
  (c) Crack?
  (d) Gang bangs?

ANSWERS: 1 — (a); 2 — (a); 3 — (c); 4 — (d).

DID YOU KNOW...?

● that Rome burned because Nero left the grill on?

● that Led Zeppelin were Mormons?

● that General Galtieri now runs a small stall on Portobello Road specialising in Art Deco knick-knacks?

● that cat-gut comes from catkins — two and a half inches per flower?

● that the only sure way to survive a fall in a barrel over Niagara Falls is to pack the barrel with molasses?

● that David Coleman was the first Doctor Who?

● that syphilis is carried by mosquitoes?

April

3

On this day in 1525 the Portuguese explorer Vasco da Gama died. He was the first man to sail from Europe to India, travelling down the coast of Africa, round the Cape of Good Hope and landing on the south-west coast of India in 1498: incredibly, he had only gone for a tin of beans.

KEVIN KEEGAN quit Newcastle United in 1984 to become the Queen's dress designer. Keegan became only the second footballer ever to fill this lucrative position: the other was full-back Alf Cohen in 1966-67.

★ ★ ★ ★ ★ ★ ★ ★ ★

THE MOST AMAZING escape ever made from Colditz during World War II was made by a Captain Henry E. Farré. Disguising himself as Eva Braun, he managed to fool guards into letting him walk out of the prison. Unfortunately, his disguise was so good that he was picked up outside by the SS and returned to Adolf Hitler. The Führer slept with Farré for three nights before realising his mistake. Farre was eventually put through a bacon slicer and his remains fed to Hitler's pet dachshund 'Panzer'.

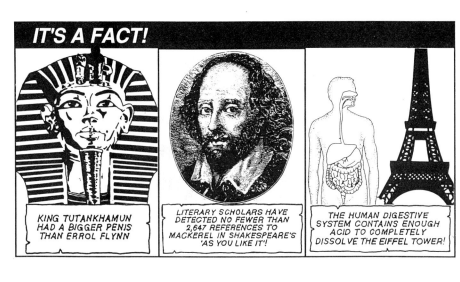

KING TUTANKHAMUN HAD A BIGGER PENIS THAN ERROL FLYNN

LITERARY SCHOLARS HAVE DETECTED NO FEWER THAN 2,647 REFERENCES TO MACKEREL IN SHAKESPEARE'S 'AS YOU LIKE IT'!

THE HUMAN DIGESTIVE SYSTEM CONTAINS ENOUGH ACID TO COMPLETELY DISSOLVE THE EIFFEL TOWER!

April
4

On this day every year a strange competition takes place on the North Yorkshire Moors. All men between the ages of sixteen and thirty-five strain to produce the largest turd or stool: the winner is then crowned 'Stool Pigeon of The Year'. The largest produced so far was in 1976 by E. Henry Ollerenshaw who produced a whopping $11\frac{1}{2}$ inch stool complete without breaks.

Did you know that the cerebellum at the back of the brain is primitive, and is the place where all your dirty words are stored?

* * * * * * * * * * * * * * *

DID YOU KNOW...?

● that the last Roman soldier left Britain in 1921?

● that when table tennis was first invented, players were allowed to serve over-arm?

● that the world's largest active volcano is situated near Cromer in Norfolk?

● that the British Telecom Tower is built on the former site of the Tower of Babel?

● that the so-called 'Bloody Assize' of 1685 was so called because Judge Jeffreys had a violent nosebleed on the first day?

● that the average hamburger has passed through the human body eighteen times?

• that criminologists have found that most founder members of terrorist organisations are disgruntled ex-Freemasons?

• that the three lanes of Spaghetti Junction are known as Tagliatelli (inside lane) Cannelloni (middle lane) and Fettuccine (fast lane)?

• that a bust of Nefertiti found in Tel-el-Amama, Egypt, proved she was a 36B cup?

• that Edward G. Robinson was a Pakistani?

• that every 31 August the French have an Eisteddfod?

Did you know that the Boston Tea Party won an Egon Ronay Award?

BIZARRE...
But TRUE!

• Sir Anthony Blunt's position in the Royal Household was 'Surveyor Of The Queen's Bob Marley Albums'!

• Marc Chagall designed the buffet at Euston Station!

• After the Second World War, Lord Haw-Haw tried to get himself a job with Radio Caroline!

• The Basque terrorists derived their name from the uniforms they wore on bombing raids — short-skirted lacy corsets!

• If there was one thing Boadicea despised more than the Romans, it was ironing!

• Euclid invented the mini-roundabout!

• The Equator passes through Aberystwyth!

On this day in 1834 the Tolpuddle Martyrs — six English labourers who tried to form a trade union — were sentenced to transportation. Before this historic event, Tolpuddle was actually called Tolpoo: when Queen Victoria asked to be informed about the circumstances surrounding the transportation, her Ministers hurriedly changed the name to Tolpuddle to avoid causing the Queen any unneccessary embarrassment. The same thing happened to Piddlehampton and Piddlehide, previously known as Poohampton and Poobottom before the Queen passed through on a visit in 1874.

DID YOU KNOW that eating turnips can cure halitosis?

THE SO-CALLED 'Greenhouse Effect', a major worry to scientists, meteorologists and botanists alike, is caused by too many tomatoes and cucumbers being grown in too small an area at any one time.

DID YOU KNOW that if you try to get into Stringfellow's with a goat before 11pm, the goat doesn't have to pay?

FREDERICK THE GREAT'S body was preserved in a jar of Marmite.

THE LARGEST piece of space debris ever to fall on Great Britain was Yuri Gagarin's flask in 1964.

DID YOU KNOW that the Universe is roughly fig-shaped?

LORD BEECHING is believed to have masterminded the 1963 Great Train Robbery. As a diversionary tactic and to avoid detection, he closed many stations and branch lines.

THE LONGEST FART in screen history occurred in the film *The Big Sleep*. Robert Mitchum broke wind unremittingly for ten minutes and fifteen seconds.

DID YOU KNOW that in some Middle Eastern countries quiche is considered to be a dangerous substance?

Did you know...?

● that Robin Hood wore khaki, not Lincoln green?

● that General Tom Thumb was 6-foot-2-inches when he was nine years old, but shrank to only 3-foot-4-inches in his adulthood?

Many British prisoners-of-war escaped from German prison camps during the Second World War, disguised as Ottoman chests.

● that there are more miles of spaghetti in Birmingham than there are in Venice?

● that Girl Guides were originally nicknamed Hell's Belles?

● that Temple Gaiting is the only hamlet in Worcestershire to have its own independent nuclear deterrent?

● that Sid Vicious was obsessed with the idea of getting a knighthood?

● that juke boxes were named after the Duke of Wellington who invented them?

● that the jock strap was originally a leather thong used for beating Highland cattle?

● that the national sport of South Africa is tossing the krugerrand?

● that Guy Fawkes's mother owned a fireworks factory in Sutton Coldfield?

April
14

On this day in 1981 the Australian National Census revealed that 87.9 per cent of the entire population shared the christian name Bruce. This unusual statistic is made even more unusual by the fact that only 48.7 per cent of the Australian population is male.

DID YOU KNOW...?

- that Denis Thatcher's pet name for Margaret is 'Boris'?

- that Rhyl is situated on top of the Oceanic Tectonic Plate and is in danger of slipping into the sea before the year 2000?

- that elephants have large gills behind their ears?

- that Pablo Picasso, before producing the work now celebrated as his 'Blue Period', had at least two Pink Periods, an Olive Period and a traumatic Brown Period?

- that Mao Tse-tung was once a pools collector for Vernons?

- that no male British tennis player has succeeded in winning the Wimbledon singles championship since the 1930s because few of them manage to progress past the strawberry tent?

- that the axolotl is the only living amphibian yet to be frightened by David Attenborough?

- that Hitler's Russian campaign in World War II was based on Arsenal's infamous offside trap of the 1940's?

IT'S A FACT!

AL CAPONE SPENT THE LAST FIVE YEARS OF HIS LIFE DOING VOLUNTARY CHARITY WORK FOR LITTLE SISTERS OF THE POOR!

May

1

On this day in 1871 the French writer Marcel Proust was born. He dictated most of work from inside a refuse skip.

- that Braille was originally invented for the deaf?

- that two-thirds of your body weight is suet?

Did you know that eighty per cent of your body heat escapes through your anus?

* * * * * * * * * * * * *

ALTHOUGH hydrogen is the most abundant element in the universe, scientists are puzzled by the fact that hardly any can be found in Norwich.

* * * * * * * * * * * * *

DID YOU KNOW that the French name for the English Channel is *Le Cut Anglais*?

* * * * * * * * * * * * *

RESEARCH has shown that MPs who take senna pods are more likely to pass a Bill than those who do not.

* * * * * * * * * * * * *

SHAKESPEARE was the first person to use the words fab, gear and groovy.

* * * * * * * * * * * * *

ALL THE BEST piano-tuners are deaf.

* * * * * * * * * * * * *

THE FIRST telephone kiosk preceded the telephone by some fifteen years.

* * * * * * * * * * * * *

THE NORTHERNMOST tip of Britain only has three hours of daylight per day during summer.

* * * * * * * * * * * * *

UNWANTED wax figures from Madame Tussauds are traditionally melted down at The Crucible Theatre, Sheffield.

* * * * * * * * * * * * *

DURING a heated Commons debate in 1985, former Tory Defence Minister Michael Heseltine grabbed the Mace and led other members of his party in a rousing chorus of 'Get 'em down, you Zulu warriors'.

* * * * * * * * * * * * *

THE RAVENS at the Tower of London are kept there because they are fed lead shot in their seed.

Did you know that Johannes Brahms got his inspiration for his chamber music by writing it inside a diving bell?

Trivia Quiz No.5

1 In John Osborne's play *Look Back in Anger*, how does the hero Jimmy Porter earn a living? Is he:
- (a) On a YTS scheme with Sketchley's the cleaners?
- (b) A Kissogram in a French Chef costume?
- (c) Chairman of the National Coal Board?
- (d) Centre-half for Raith Rovers?

2 The Beatles gave their last ever concert at Candlestick Park, San Francisco, on 29 August 1966. What was behind the Fab Four's unusual decision to stop touring? Was it:
- (a) Because George suffered from travel sickness?
- (b) Because John had recently become a Jehovah's Witness, and this was causing friction between him and Paul?
- (c) Because the crowds had stopped coming: contrary to popular belief they were considered passé by 1966; in fact, at their last gig only 15 people turned up to watch?
- (d) Because Ringo wanted babies?

3 By what nickname were Sir Matt Busby's Manchester United teams fondly remembered in the 1950s and 1960s? Were they:
- (a) The Red Arrows?
- (b) The Red Brigade?
- (c) The Khmer Rouge?
- (d) The Ton-Ton Macoute?

4 Who was the first Doctor Who? Was it:
- (a) Howard Keel?
- (b) Sidney Poitier
- (c) Alastair Burnet?
- (d) Moira Anderson?

5 Which of the following has Elizabeth Taylor never been married to? Was it:
- (a) Patrick Moore?
- (b) 'Baby Doc' Duvalier?
- (c) The West Midlands Gas Board?
- (d) Plymouth Argyle FC?

ANSWERS: 1 — (c); 2 — (a); 3 — (a); 4 — (b); 5 — (c).

May 10

On this day in 1340 the poet Geoffrey Chaucer was born. He was the first court poet to write in his native English rather than Latin, and his *Canterbury Tales* became the basis of modern English literature. He dedicated all of his spare time to creating and cataloguing unusual and exotic underwear: Chaucer himself wrote that he had 'a partycular lykynge for fplit-crotch pantyf'.

Humphrey Bogart: once surprised leading lady Lauren Bacall during a
tender love scene by eating his duvet.

Britain's most verified sighting of a UFO was at a transvestite convention near Basingstoke in 1953

DURING the Cuban crisis of 1963 US spy satellites located vast numbers of Fidel Castro look-alikes stockpiled on the island.

PABLO PICASSO used to keep warm when he was a young, poor, struggling and unknown painter by burning some of his friends.

DID YOU KNOW that the wind which blows through Tottenham Court Road tube station is known as *le mistral*?

March
14

On this day every year thousands of gnus begin their annual migration to Britain. Not many survive the treacherous trip from the African grasslands, however: most do not understand that they have to get aboard a ferry to cross the Channel, and drown at Calais.

Did You Know...?

● that a shoal of hungry goldfish is more dangerous than the Great White Shark?

● that Wigan is sometimes called 'Little Paris'?

● that the most common christian name in China is Brian?

● that Quasimodo, the hunchback of Notre-Dame, suffered from 'Dowager's Hump'?

● that in mediaeval times a codpiece was exactly what the name implies — a portion of cod tied to one's groin?

● that Alton Priors is the only village in Wiltshire ruled by a military junta?

● that Al Jolson really was black?

● that when 'Lord' Howard Carter opened the tomb of Tutankhamun, he found amongst the treasures ten Woodbine?

● that Richard Nixon now lives in Purley?

● that in 200 AD Hartlepool was bigger than either Rome or Jerusalem?

● that the Chinese celebrate Hogmanay?

● ●

THE FIRST steam iron was half as big again as Brunel's SS *Great Britain.*

●

IN SPITE OF her austere image, Queen Victoria enjoyed a rather risqué line in underwear. She often wore black stockings with red suspenders, small frilly crotchless crinolene panties and peephole bras with tassles.

●

WOOLLY MAMMOTHS were still alive in Charles Dickens' day: he made three references to them in *The Old Curiosity Shop.*

●

RICHARD ARKWRIGHT (1732–92) helped revolutionise the Lancashire cotton industry when he stumbled upon the idea of harnessing two Rolls-Royce jet engines to an ordinary broad handloom.

On this day in 1890 Charles de Gaulle was born, a French general and statesman who led the Free French movement after the fall of France in 1940 and became President of his country twice. During the Algerian crisis he lay in a hole in his garden for an entire day for no apparent reason.

Did you know…?

- that Cairn terriers are considered sacred in Hull?

- that during an average night's sleep, humans lose up to two gallons of body fluid?

- that watching snooker is a major cause of hair loss?

- that the koala bear is an even more formidable adversary than the polar bear, and can kill a man with one blow of its tiny paw?

✴ ✴ ✴ ✴ ✴ ✴ ✴ ✴ ✴

THE ZIEGFELD FOLLIES were a series of gazebos, summer-houses and false ruins built by Samuel E. Ziegfeld across France to cover up the mess left by the Maginot Line, which had been created as a defence against German infantry during World War I. The Arc de Triomphe and the Eiffel Tower are both fine examples of Ziegfeld's work.

✴

EDWARD JENNER discovered a cure for cowpox, but caught smallpox in the process!

✴

DID YOU KNOW that porcupines are particularly prone to attacks of 'pins and needles'?

✴

The famous composer Felix Bartholdy Mendelssohn. Did you know that he suffered from a compulsion to write treble clefs on toilet walls?

Did you know that most of the Beatles' hits were written by Yoko Ono?

DID YOU KNOW that the Hanging Gardens of Babylon contained no fewer than 4,500 garden gnomes?

COAL is formed by compressed layers of rotting fish, built up over thousands of years. Thick seams of fish are to be found under much of the British countryside, particularly Nottinghamshire, Durham and South Wales.

MAHATMA GANDHI was a keen sportsman during his days at an English public school. His ideas on passive resistance, however, got him thrown out of his house tug-o'-war team.

THE GRIZZLY BEAR is the world's largest aphid.

*

DID YOU KNOW that Tooting Broadway was built by the Druids?

*

SIR FRANCIS DRAKE was captain of his local bowls team, the Plymouth Armadas. Drake took his team to league championships for three successive seasons and was said to have an exceptional eye for a jack. The great irony was that three members of his team were Spanish.

* * * * * * * * * * * * * *

● The French Resistance confused German occupying forces during the latter part of World War II by masterminding seventeen different escape routes from Oldham to Hamburg.

MAZING...
But TRUE!

- The Victoria Cross is made out of soup tureens captured from Russians during the Battle of Balaclava.

•

- A favourite hobby of the ancient Egyptians was philately.

- The Iron Bridge in Shropshire was built by the Anglo-Saxons and lay forgotten until the Industrial Revolution.

- Maundy Thursday is the day on which the Queen traditionally distributes token miniatures of spirits among commuters on the Charing Cross Underground.

•

- Marconi's only subsequent invention to the wireless transmitter was the hula hoop.

•

- A male elephant contains enough body fluid to wash an average Australian family for one year.

•

- The first person to bring Christianity to Suffolk was St Nigel.

Did you know that Prince Philip's 'local' is The Magpie & Stump, King's Road, Chelsea? He is president of the pub skittles 'B' team, but only in an honorary capacity as he never actually plays.

On this day in 1939 Sigmund Freud, the Austrian doctor who founded psychoanalysis, died. His last words on his deathbed were 'There's nowt so queer as folk'.

• The Aztecs founded a wealthy civilisation in South America based on the manufacture and export of Tupperware.

• Herrings are the only salt-water fish to suffer from alopecia — although the large halibut often has recurring dandruff problems.

• Charlie Chaplin's legs were bowed because he had rickets.

• Reginald Mitchell's maternal uncle Hans was awarded The Blue Max during the First World War.

• Freckles are caused by tiny imperfections in the Earth's ozone layer which allow too much ultra-violet light to pass through.

• Forty-seven tsars are buried alongside Karl Marx in Highgate Cemetery.

• Human beings shed up to 3 hundredweight of dry skin every day.

• Kangaroos chew eucalyptus leaves in order to cure severe head colds.

• The sabre-toothed tiger was wiped out by Legionnaire's Disease.

Did You Know...?

• that Ming china comes from Ming, North Staffordshire?

• that the stratosphere contains millions of tiny tea leaves?

• that King Arthur's fabled Round Table is now in the Cabinet Room of No. 10 Downing Street?

• that there is a short cut from Land's End to John O'Groats via Wales which is only 47 miles long?

• that the cox of the winning Boat Race crew is awarded a fox's brush?

• that a single mushroom contains six hundred calories?

• that panama hats originated in Blackpool?

Trivia Quiz No.6

1 Who remarked that genius was 'one per cent inspiration and ninety-nine per cent perspiration'? Was it:
  (a) Albert Einstein?
  (b) Vidal Sassoon?
  (c) Jocky Wilson?
  (d) Eric Bristow?

2 In the BBC children's programme, what were Andy Pandy's two friends called? Were they:
  (a) Nina and Frederick?
  (b) Sonny and Cher?
  (c) Jekyll and Hyde?
  (d) Burke and Hare?

3 What three inventions, according to Francis Bacon, have changed the world since classical times? Were they:
  (a) Y-Fronts, pot noodles and the wah-wah pedal?
  (b) Loons, natural gas and heated rollers?
  (c) Screw-in football studs, Tipp-Ex and sanitary towels?
  (d) Sandwich toasters, dandruff-control shampoo and the moped?

4. Where was Mark Thatcher travelling from, and where was he driving to, when he became hopelessly lost in the Sahara desert in 1984? Was it:
  (a) From Cleethorpes to Basildon?
  (b) From Stevenage to Weymouth: he took a wrong turn at Sutton Scotney?
  (c) From Reigate to Guildford: he had a bit of a mucky windscreen and his washer bottle was empty?
  (d) From Huyton to Salford: he was confused by the contraflow system on the M62?

5 Bill and Ben were children's TV characters, The Flowerpot Men. What was the name of their friend who lived between them? Was it:
  (a) Grass?
  (b) Coke?
  (c) Smack?
  (d) Crack?

ANSWERS: 1 — (c); 2 — (a); 3 — (d); 4 — (d); 5 — (a).

Did You Know...?

● that goats are dyslexic?

● that Eric Bristow's wardrobe for the 1987 World Professional Darts Championship was created by Teddy Tinling?

● that John Constable loathed Suffolk?

● that every Friday the Duke of Edinburgh visits each member of the Royal Family to collect their pools money?

- that Basil Brush's very first co-star was Clint Eastwood?

- that Picasso's *Les Demoiselles d'Avignon* was painted at Lambeth Bridge?

- that Mussolini's favourite opening gambit was 'Hello, my darlings'?

- that the Pantheon in Paris was decorated by E. L. Greckott & Sons, Sheen?

- that the most-used word in the English language is 'fish'?

- that the very mention of AIDS is taboo in some countries: in Australia it is euphemistically referred to as 'Foster's', 'Devil's Thingy' or 'Bruce's Syndrome'?

- that the Romans had micros and VDUs but rejected them on the grounds that they were useless?

- that The Shadows' famous 'three-step-and-kick' stage routine was choreographed by Margot Fonteyn?

- that Lady Hamilton had a brief fling with Napoleon?

- that Halley's Comet has a McDonald's on it?

- that the Chancellor of the Exchequer has a pet chameleon called Noel that changes colour on budget day?

- that ANZAC Day is a national holiday in Japan?

- that heart transplant pioneer Dr Christian Barnard had a pair of 'lucky' Marigolds?

- that Lawrence of Arabia had a fear of sand?

- that Country and Western music has its roots in old Norwegian fishing songs?

- that in many remote parts of northern Scotland the haggis is worshipped as a god?

- that the Princess of Wales's favourite group is Motorhead?

- that Aristotle's real name was Harry Stottle?

- that the role of Minnie Caldwell in *Coronation Street* was played by Meryl Streep?

- that cod are actually born in batter?

- that Jules Verne's head was no longer than a peach?

- that the Mafia were originally from Guernsey?

- that to keep their hair spiky, punks use a mixture of dung, rancid yak fat and plaster of Paris?

May

25

On this day in 1940 thousands of British and Allied troops escaped from the beaches of Dunkirk disguised as travelling Hoover salesmen.

Nostradamus – Some Of His Lesser Known Predictions

The legendary French seer Nostradamus made many uncanny predictions, including the rise of Adolf Hitler and Napoleon Bonaparte. But did you know that he also predicted:

- The Cecil Parkinson affair!
- Prawn-cocktail flavoured crisps!
- Rubik's Cube!
- Ian Rush!
- The entire Wimbledon promotion-winning team of 1986, including their substitutes!
- Flared trousers!
- Richard Clayderman!
- Cavity wall insulation!
- Ursula Andress's bust size!
- *Brookside*!

* * * * * * * * * * * * * *

DUE TO THE earth's rotation, th M1, M5 and M6 motorways all shift to the right by one inch every year.

* * * * * * * * * * * * * *

June 18

On this day in 856, Viking hordes led by Erik Bloodaxe began a series of ruthless assaults on the English coastline. Contrary to the popular myth, Vikings were nearly always vegetarian. Bloodaxe's favourite dish was aubergine lasagne, whereas Hrolf the Ganger and Erik the Red preferred low-calorie lentil dips followed by courgette-and-mung-bean pie.

IT'S A FACT!

WHEN HE WAS A YOUNG MAN AT SANDHURST WINSTON CHURCHILL INVENTED THE 'GOOSE STEP'!

IN 1874 WALTER M. DONG OF BOSTON, U.S.A. MANUFACTURED AN ABRASIVE TOILET PAPER FOR MASOCHISTS!

NAPOLEON HAD HIS NAME CHANGED BY DEED POLL BECAUSE HE DIDN'T THINK THAT HIS REAL NAME 'NEVILLE' WAS THAT OF A TRUE LEADER!

THE LONGEST RIVER in the world is the mighty River Yarty in South Devon. Although an initial glance at a map may suggest that the Amazon or Nile are considerably longer, length is purely a matter of definition. The Yarty is connected to the River Dart, which in turn is connected to the upper reaches of the River Severn. The Severn in turn is connected by an underground stream to the River Trent, which also happens to be connected to the Mersey via the small Abbey Brook. The Mersey is connected by its headwaters to the River Derwent, which joins the River Ribble. The Ribble runs underground to resurface at the Ouse near York, only to disappear and then resurface over the border in Scotland as a small burn called College Burn. The burn flows to a series of lochs before reappearing as Whiteadder Water near the Firth of Forth. This then leads to the River Isla, the Water of Tarf, the Water of Buchat, the Water of Nochty, the Burn of Rothes, the quaintly named Abhain an t'Strath Chuileannaich, Loch Choire Mhoir, Lock Shin, the River Mallart, Loch An Alltain Fhearna and the River Dyke before finally (and exhaustingly, for anyone who may attempt to canoe this mighty stretch of water) reaching the sea at Uair Strathy near Strathy Point at the northernmost tip of Scotland. In all therefore the Yarty is approximately 7,000 miles long, 3,000 miles longer than the Amazon.

• • • • • • • • •

THE GARDEN OF EDEN referred to in *Genesis* 3 is generally held to have been situated in Stoke-on-Trent.

EASTER ISLAND is famous for the tall stone busts of Clodagh Rodgers which gaze mysteriously out to sea.

DID YOU KNOW that London has twelve exclusively gay hot-dog stalls?

JIMI HENDRIX'S song 'All Along The Watchtower' was loosely based on George Formby's 'When I'm Cleaning Windows', although Formby's publishing company never actually sued.

HARA KIRI is not an exclusively Japanese phenomenon: until the 1950s it was considered honourable for incompetent British civil servants to hurl themselves onto their fountain pens. This custom died out largely because of the advent of felt-tip pens.

IDI AMIN, exiled former ruler of Uganda, is now the part-time lead singer of a Bristol-based skiffle band. In 1986 Idi and The Hep-Cats completed a twenty-five-day tour of West Country working-men's clubs.

CUMULUS CLOUDS actually contain 20 per cent cotton wool.

• • • • • • • •

DID YOU KNOW that the only thing that Aristotle never philosophised about was his feet?

NUCLEAR WAR–DON'T WORRY!

- Top experts now agree that if a 10,000-megaton bomb was to be dropped on Birmingham, the effects five miles away would be minimal!

- A 1,000-megaton bomb would not even blow off the roof of your house, even with a direct hit!

- After a nuclear attack, some people may experience a minor tummy upset — but not in all cases. Have some Beecham's powders handy, or, better still, a small bottle of kaolin and morphine!

- There would be a soothing, gentle breeze to follow!

★ ★ ★

DID YOU KNOW that the Queen likes to wear her crown around Buckingham Palace even when she is washing up?

★ ★ ★

June
21

On this day every year the young bulls of Pamplona are allowed to run freely through the Bull Ring Shopping Centre in Birmingham.

- People caught out in the open during an attack may acquire a slight suntan: very attractive when worn with white clothing!

- You may see a bright light — very pretty to look at!

- A light dust would descend, but this could be hoovered up with any domestic vacuum cleaner!

- Some people may experience slight soreness of the gums and perhaps a little bleeding. Ask your dentist to recommend a softer toothbrush: after a couple of days these nasty effects will disappear!

* * * * * * * * * * * * * *

THE WORLD'S 10 MOST DESIRABLE MEN

1   David Coleman
2   Rolf Harris
3   Sir Geoffrey Howe
4   Desmond Lynam
5   Patrick Moore
6   Lionel Blair
7   Kenny Dalgleish
8   Barry Took
9   Michael Fish
10 Denis Thatcher

* * * * * * * * * * * * * *

THE HALLÉ ORCHESTRA depend entirely upon the spoons for their percussion section.

THE SPEAKER'S CHAIR in the House of Commons is a milkmaid's stool rescued from a barn in Somerset in 1793.

Trivia Quiz No.7

1 What does a milophobe suffer from? Is it:
   (a) A fear of millepedes?
   (b) A fear of millionaires?
   (c) A fear of Millicent Martin?
   (d) A fear of the Milk Marketing Board?

2 What, according to the account of the Sermon on the Mount in the New Testament, did you have to be to enable you to enter the Kingdom of Heaven? Was it:
   (a) Over 5 foot 10 inches?
   (b) A Freemason?
   (c) An American Express card-holder?
   (d) Dead?

3 Which TV personality is famous for his catchphrase 'Not a lot of people know that!'? Is it:
   (a) Bamber Gascoigne?
   (b) Magnus Magnusson?
   (c) Patrick Moore?
   (d) A.J.P. Taylor?

4 Who wrote the best-seller *Kane and Abel*? Was it:
   (a) Dostoevsky?
   (b) Muddy Waters?
   (c) Bill Sirs?
   (d) Bert Millichip?

5 The British and Commonwealth Heavyweight Boxing Championship was vacated by Frank Bruno. But who is the current holder? Is it:
   (a) Tiny Rowland?
   (b) David Essex?
   (c) Boy George?
   (d) Petula Clarke?

ANSWERS: 1 — (d); 2 — (a); 3 — (c); 4 — (a); 5 — (d).

Richard Wagner, 1813–1883. Did you know that his romantic opera *The Flying Dutchman* had a 'Party Mix', a 'Street Mix' and a 'Cheeky Mix?'

DID YOU KNOW...?

● that Dylan Thomas liked to flagellate himself with a leek?

● that the official residence of the Queen Mother is Lipton's of Ashbourne?

- that in the TV series, Batman's sidekick Robin was originally played by Sir Alec Guinness?

- that Ferdinand de Lesseps engineered Rotherham Municipal Baths?

- that in 1986 the Russians commissioned two thousand hanging baskets for the East German side of the Berlin Wall?

- that the capital of Peru is Doncaster?

- that The Ashes competed for by English and Australian cricket teams are those of Jack Hobbs?

- that the traditional native costume worn by Zulu warriers were Fred Perry T-Shirts?

- that a single hamster on a treadmill could generate enough electricity to supply the whole of New York?

- that Eva Peron was plagued by excess facial hair and had to shave at least three times a week?

- that lemmings cheat — they catch a thermal and glide?

- that cricketer W. G. Grace always kept a copy of *Wisden* concealed in his beard?

- that the effects of gravity are felt less at Chipping Sodbury than anywhere else in the world?

July

14

On this day in 1779 Thomas Chippendale died. Although Chippendale's name became synonymous with fine and expensive furniture, he in fact spent his entire lifetime making and repairing deck chairs.

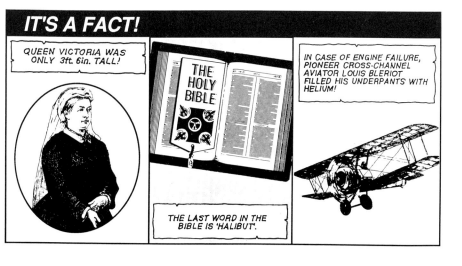

IT'S A FACT!

QUEEN VICTORIA WAS ONLY 3ft. 6in. TALL!

THE HOLY BIBLE

THE LAST WORD IN THE BIBLE IS 'HALIBUT'.

IN CASE OF ENGINE FAILURE, PIONEER CROSS-CHANNEL AVIATOR LOUIS BLERIOT FILLED HIS UNDERPANTS WITH HELIUM!

DID YOU KNOW...?

- that on his way to the summit of Everest in 1985, Chris Bonington threw a Tupperware party on the south col?

- that only minutes before her execution Anne Boleyn complained of a migraine?

- that there was only ever one Egyptian pharoah who was British: Cecil Rameses III?

- that Capability Brown had his own allotment?

- that the Milky Way contains no more than 116 stars?

- that Karl Marx was thrown out of the Monday Club because of his appalling table manners? He wrote *Das Kapital* to get his own back.

July
17

On this day in 1966 the Norwegian parliament was forced to cancel its summer recess because of a sudden plague of dwarf canaries.

- that if Great Britain was just one degree further north it would be impossible to obtain a sun tan here even in summer?

- that clouds are heavier than lead?

- that photographic X-rays of Leonardo da Vinci's masterpiece *The Last Supper* reveal that a mousse, three jugglers, a grand piano and several crates of brown ale had been painted out on the Pope's instructions?

- that Augustus invented the 'calendar method'?

BRITAIN'S MOST dangerous sport is croquet: last year there were over 700 serious injuries, ove 4,000 minor injuries and seven deaths.

FIFTY-NINE of the USA's 2,000 different religious denominations believe that Bob Geldof is God. Even allowing for the Americans' apparent eagerness to latch on to diverse and often freaky causes, this statistic is particularly unusual, since fifty-seven of these groups were founded when Bob was still a humble Boomtown Rat and had yet even to think of raising money for famine relief. In actual church attendance figures, however, Geldof worshippers are still outnumbered by devotees of the Church of the Sacred Bleeding Heart of Bruce Springsteen.

Great Moments in Science No. 1

• • • • • • • • • •

PEELERS WERE so called because they often peeled their clothes off when faced with a particularly nasty criminal.

• • • • • • • • • •

Great Moments in Science No. 2

Great Moments in Science No. 3

Great Moments in Science No. 4

GREAT MOMENTS IN SCIENCE:

Fig 1 — The first microchip.
Fig 2 — Professor Wilhelm von Röntgen investigates the long-term effect of radiation upon cheeseburgers.

Fig 3 — Rutherford's early work on splitting the atom. Fig 4 — Gilchrist and Thomas patent a 'weak' home-perming solution.

SOME PREDICTIONS YET

TO BE BORNE OUT

- That a man called Noel Edmonds will one day become the fifth James Bond.
- That in 1995 a man called Lord David Sutch will head a Monster Raving Loony Party/SDP/Liberal Coalition Government.
- That a football team called Crewe Alexandra will win the European Cup four times in succession.
- That a man called Elvis Costello will one day win the Eurovision Song Contest.
- That a man called Michael Fish will one day become the ninth husband of Elizabeth Taylor.
- That a mighty city will rise, architecturally supreme, and that it will be called Milton Keynes.
- That a virulent disease will sweep the world, causing brain damage to all who catch it, resulting in total loss of intelligent conversation, and that the disease will be known as 'Soap'.
- That an impoverished brown-skinned people will break free from the shackles of their oppressors, rise from the West like a mighty tide and conquer the world, and that they will be Cornish.
- That a powerful American family will yield four great sons who will seek high office, that two will become Presidents of their country, that two will be assassinated, one while he is President and one while running for the Presidency, and that their names will be Groucho, Chico, Harpo and Zeppo.

August
25

On this day in 1772 the poet Samuel Taylor Coleridge was born, author of *The Rime of the Ancient Mariner.* The original draft of his poem shows that Coleridge clearly intended to have a budgerigar as the bird of doom: his publisher, however, had recently lost a much cherished pet budgie and Coleridge changed the bird to an albatross rather than risk upsetting him.

DID YOU KNOW that the French do not have a word for dandruff? Consequently they never suffer from it?

AUSTRALIAN DOCTORS now recognise that alcoholism as a prime cause of lost working hours is second only to sheep-sniffing.

UNDER CERTAIN climatic conditions, guppies can turn into far more ferocious killers than piranhas or even barracuda.

APRIL FOOL was a real woman who loved to play dastardly tricks on people in London in the seventeenth century.

DID YOU KNOW that you can counteract the effects of nuclear fallout by eating lamb chops?

A SINGLE grain of rice, if boiled constantly for seven and a half hours, would swell so dramatically that it would be large enough to feed the entire population of the Isle of Man for a day.

NEW MEMBERS of the House of Lords are ceremonially presented with their own personal rubber cushion.

EDWARD the fourteenth-century Prince of Wales, was known as 'the Black Prince' because he never once washed throughout his lifetime: even a contemporary engraving of his investiture shows him to have muddy knees and dirty feet.

● Rudolph Valentino died celibate.

Mr Rodney Stoats set an unusual world record on 14 May 1987, when he became the first man ever to swim the full length of Sellafield beach, from St Bees Head to Ravenglass, twenty times.

Did You Know...?

- that the staple diet of Sudan is cheesecake?

- that a warthog can have as many as 1,000 warts on its bum?

- that a cheeseplant, given the right conditions, can yield up to seven pounds of Edam?

- that Dracula's creator, Bram Stoker, died from severe love bites?

- that the first English banknote was bigger than a tablecloth?

- that Crewe railway station is built on the site of a former Roman chariot depot?

- that acid rain falling on Keighley, Yorkshire, has caused premature baldness in a Lady Mayoress?

- that the traditional Turkish greeting is copulation?

- that Britain's biggest spectator sport is frog-taunting?

- that The Hundred Years War only lasted a fortnight?

- that Wyatt Earp was awarded the first-ever Nobel Peace Prize?

- that the earth is reckoned at most to be 4,000 years old?

- that there are 164 references to haggis in the Bible?

- that Lenin's tomb is covered in seashells?

- • • • • • • • •

- that Tory 'wets' were so-called because they were incontinent?

- that the Saxons used to dye their hair blond?

- that Christopher Columbus discovered the Channel Islands?

August
29

On this day in 1986 an auction of Beatle memorabilia was held at Christie's. John Lennon's prize winning cactus collection fetched an astonishing £4,000.

Trivia Quiz No.8

1 What does an MP do when 'filibustering'? Is it:
   (a) A wolf whistle: male Members employ it as a chauvinist tactic to embarrass and patronise female Members when they are addressing the House?

(b) The House of Commons equivalent of the 'human wave' seen at stadiums during the Los Angeles Olympics and the World Cup: Members use it as a sign of approval for a particularly good Bill?

(c) A 'raspberry', traditionally blown *en masse* by backbenchers at the government of the day at the start of Prime Minister's Question Time?

(d) A high-pitched 'ni!' sound traditionally made by the Opposition as they go to vote after the Division Bell has sounded?

2 Which site in Britain has a mystical significance for Druids on Midsummer Eve? Is it:
(a) Rotherham Municipal Baths?
(b) Clapham North tube station?
(c) The Ideal Home Exhibition?
(d) The Gas Showroom, Wapping?

3 What was Carl Gustav Jung famous for?
(a) Snooker's first televised maximum break?
(b) He founded Virgin Records?

(c) He invented pasteurised milk?
(d) He was the original 'Bubbles' in the painting by Sir John Millais used for Pear's Soap advertisements?

4 What unfortunate physical deformity did Anne Boleyn possess? Was it:
(a) Twelve toes and two navels?
(b) Sixteen fingers, twelve toes and three livers?
(c) Three buttocks and a tail?
(d) No head?

5 Of which trade is St Crispin traditionally the patron saint? Is it:
(a) Chartered accountancy?
(b) Systems analysis?
(c) Data processing?
(d) Quantity surveying?

ANSWERS: 1 — (b); 2 — (d); 3 — (d); 4 — (d); 5 — (a).

* * * * * * * * * * * * * * *

DID YOU KNOW that on some of our older major roads the cat's-eyes are prone to conjunctivitis?

SELLAFIELD NUCLEAR power station is so safe that you could stand inside a reactor full of fuel rods without suffering any harmful effects.

COLLECTIVISM IS a term used to describe the hobbies of stamp collectors, beer mat collectors, postcard collectors, etc. The word was first coined by Mikhail Bukanin who described himself as a 'collectivist anarchist': to prove his point he publicly destroyed an entire collection of rare birds' eggs he had accumulated since he was seven years old.

10 MOST ENDURING SAYINGS OF ROBBIE BURNS

1   'Och, this porridge is tae lumpy.'
2   'Stitch this, Jimmy.'
3   'Ma bastard Giro's nae arrived.'
4   'Hae are you staring at, Jimmy?'
5   'I'll mebbe neck some heavy and dae a wee bit o' scrutting.'
6   'I'm nae feeling virry weel.'
7   'Can ye smell gas?'
8   'They dinnae sleep taegither.'
9   'Och, it's wet rain.'
10 'Sit on ma face an' I'll teach ye hae tae yodel, lass.'

On this day in 1666 the Great Fire of London began. It was started at a bakery in Pudding Lane by Samuel Pepys in order to give himself something to write about.

DID YOU KNOW...?

● that the iceberg which sank the *Titanic* went down with her?

● that 'Glam Rock' is so-called because it originated in Glamorganshire?

● that Lord Denning used to disrupt debates in the House of Lords by doing his impression of a trim-phone?

● that Torremolinos was once a penal colony?

● that Lenin liked to play polo?

● that the African muntjac is the most prudish mammal in the animal kingdom — it never mates?

● that Leonardo da Vinci invented loft-lagging?

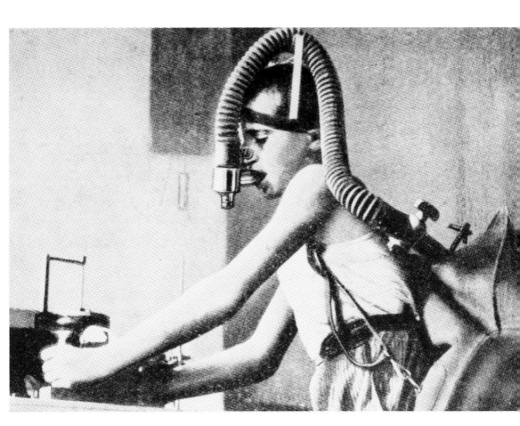

In the state of Georgia, USA, the common punishment for people caught committing minor offences is to force them to smell their own gases.

● ● ● ● ● ● ● ● ●

● that John the Baptist enjoyed having his feet anointed with Tizer?

● that the London Underground's Piccadilly Line was designed by Sir Christopher Wren?

● that Sherpa Tensing was so called because he tended to 'freeze up' at a particularly critical moment of a climb?

● that the Pentagon is really a trapezium?

● that Accrington comprises 38 different cantons?

● that Keith Moon, Janis Joplin and Eric Clapton are all former timpanists with the Hallé Orchestra?

● that Agatha Christie started as a store detective at Lewis's?

● that in Trinidad it is considered fashionable to flaunt one's colostomy bag?

● ● ● ● ● ● ● ●

THE OTTOMAN EMPIRE stretched from Rhyl in north Wales right down to Tenby in the south, Wrexham in the east and Barmouth in the west.

ALBERT EINSTEIN'S work on the Theory of Relativity was so poorly paid that he was forced to supplement his income by taking a part time van driving job with Alpine Soft Drinks.

* * * * * * * * * * * * * *

THE FIRST CAVE PAINTINGS discovered at Lascaux and Altimira depicted Graeme Souness being sent off for spitting during a Scotland 'friendly' against France.

* * * * * * * * * * * * * *

THE HANGING GARDENS OF BABYLON got their name after seventeen slave gardeners accidentally ruined a petunia bed in 1705 BC. For their crime they were hanged by the neck from tall elderberry bushes.

September

28

On this day in 1879 the last wild wolf in England was slaughtered on the London Underground at Charing Cross Station.

GIRAFFES are one of the few tree-climbing mammals which do not build nests. Instead they prefer to lie in shallow holes in the ground covered with tarpaulin remnants.

* * * * * * * * * * * * * *

IT'S A FACT!

EVIL GESTAPO BOSS HEINRICH HIMMLER ENCOURAGED INMATES OF HIS NAZI EXTERMINATION CAMPS TO PARTICIPATE IN QUALITY CIRCLES!

Did You Know...?

● that Salford is known as the Big Apple?

● that the Halifax 'loop line' is a folly? It leads to nowhere in particular — only back on itself.

● that the average age of people on the Scilly Isles is ninety-four?

● that the English Pre-Raphaelite artist Sir John Millais was only three years old when he died?

● that the Nobel Peace Prize is actually a Selfridges food hamper?

● that the moon is an optical illusion?

● that computers were originally no bigger than cigarette packets but have increased in size over the years?

● that Britain's best surfing conditions are to be found along the Trent/Mersey Canal?

● that Catherine the Great invented tampons?

● that elephants hibernate?

● that the Slav alphabet comprises only two letters?

● that the most popular Christian name for a Chilean woman is Madge?

● that Caligula once poisoned his pet terrapin because he thought it was poised to take over Rome?

LEVELS OF *HARMLESS* BACKGROUND RADIATION FOUND IN EVERYDAY OBJECTS

TV Sets	— 1 rad
Curtains	— 1 rad
Cheese	— 1 rad
False teeth	— 2 rads
Toupees	— 2 rads
Eggplants	— 3 rads
Sellotape	— 3 rads
Scones	— 4 rads
Panty-hose	— 4 rads
Surgical appliances	— 4 rads
Damart thermal vests	— 5 rads
Bed linen	— 6 rads
Duvets (single)	— 7 rads
Duvets (king size)	— 14 rads
Baked beans	— 16 rads
Tinned spaghetti	— 17 rads
Custard powder	— 18 rads
Radiators	— 100 rads
Radishes	— 1000 rads

Trivia Quiz No.9

1 Sellafield is famed for its beneficial spa water. TRUE or FALSE?

2 Arsenal Football Club are nicknamed 'The Duvets'. TRUE or FALSE?

3 Charles Dickens's novel *David Copperfield* contains no fewer than 2,439 spelling mistakes. TRUE or FALSE?

4 Madonna met Sean Penn on Cilla Black's TV show *Blind Date*. TRUE or FALSE?

5 In 1981 Charlton Heston was nominated for an Oscar for Best Toupee. TRUE or FALSE?

6 David Bowie keeps pigeons. TRUE or FALSE?

7 Francis Ford Coppola once went £6 million over budget on a TV dog food commercial. TRUE or FALSE?

8 The Duchess of York is licensed to drive a Heavy Goods Vehicle. TRUE or FALSE?

9 The Beatles' *White Album* was written entirely by Yoko Ono. TRUE or FALSE?

10 Phil Collins was a Munchkin in *The Wizard of Oz*. TRUE or FALSE?

ANSWERS: 1 — (b); 2 — (a); 3 — (a); 4 — (c); 5 — (e); 6 — (b); 7 — (c); 8 — (a); 9 — (d); 10 — (d).

Did You Know...?

● that in the Middle Ages scholars believed that the anus was the seat of intelligence?

● that Dartmoor ponies eat 2 pounds of granite daily to provide roughage in their diet?

● that George Stephenson's 'Rocket' still holds the record as the fastest ever train?

● that people entering the Taj Mahal are only allowed to wear trainers?

● that photographs sent back by the space probe Voyager II show that Venus is inhabited by poodles?

● that weatherman Michael Fish runs a trout farm?

● that there are no floors or ceilings in Centrepoint?

● that the English language originated in Peru?

● that Bob Geldof was voted Best Dressed Man by readers of the *Radio Times* in 1985?

● that singer Tom Jones was thrown out of the Welsh Eisteddfodd for being too 'raunchy'?

● that Salvador Dali liked to use a live ostrich for an easel?

● that Noah's wife was named Brenda?

● that Rodin's real name was Ron Dirn?

● that Sinn Fein, translated literally, means jacket potato?

● that bran can give you worms?

● that Nell Gwynne was a Russian spy?

October

9

On this day every year the Church of England clergy play a conker championship. The games are taken very seriously, and three bishops in recent years have been excommunicated for cheating. Former Archbishop of Canterbury, Dr Ramsey once boasted a 'thirty-niner'.

● that Mao Tse-tung's famous 'Long March' of 1934 was from Kiangsi to Stourbridge?

● that according to a recent poll, there are only three remaining families in Great Britain who don't own a video recorder?

● that for more than twenty years Joseph of Aramathea used the Holy Shroud of Turin as a loose cover?

CHARLES DICKENS WAS DYSLEXIC!

VICTORIAN POET LAUREATE ALFRED LORD TENNYSON WROTE OVER 250 SONNETS ABOUT HIS BOTTOM!

ISAMBARD KINGDOM BRUNEL BUILT THREE PAPIER MACHÉ BRIDGES ACROSS THE RIVER AVON BEFORE ATTEMPTING A STEEL ONE!

THE VAN ALLEN BELTS are a unique collection of wide, thin, long, and short buckled belts owned by Herbert Van Allen, Pennsylvania, USA.

October
25

On this day in 1799 the French novelist Honoré de Balzac was born. He wrote endless novels about snails, including *Sexy L'Escargot* (1826), *Eugène The Snail* (1833), *Snail de Chagrin* (1834), '*L'Escargot Et Moï* (1835), and *J'Aime Mes Escargots* (1836). His only diversification, *Le Frog et le Lit Solitaire* (1837) was a complete critical failure and caused him to paint himself green and live out the remaining thirteen years of his life in a potting-shed.

Did You Know..?

● that Jesus was able to feed the 5,000 with only five barley loaves and two small fishes because he was adept at cutting very thin sandwiches?

● that in 1982 Tintagel, Cornwall, was 'twinned' with Moscow?

● that Joan Crawford was originally cast in the role of Tarzan until Johnny Weismuller won his Olympic Gold Medals?

● that the Thames Barrier is made of sponge?

● that a plagiarist is someone who sets out deliberately to catch other people's diseases?

● that there were thirteen disciples, not twelve? St Barry was thrown out because his name didn't sound religious enough.

● that Josef Stalin was a stand-up comic in Russian vaudeville during the early 1900s?

- that the *Bismarck* was originally a coal barge on the Salford Ship Canal before she became the pride of the German Navy?

- that the contraceptive pill is a placebo?

- that Sir Walter Raleigh smoked sixty a day?

- that Red Indians invented fish and chips?

- that for Tibetan Priests, the holiest place in the world is Macclesfield?

- that if you travel north of Watford you have to put your clocks back one hour?

- that Hippocrates caught mumps eight times?

- that there are fifteen different types of whale in the River Thames?

- that in terms of life insurance, the most dangerous job in the world is chartered accountancy?

- that if your tonsils grow too large they will suffocate you?

- that Henry VIII's second wife was Priscilla Presley?

- that the Taiwanese have bred a sheep capable of producing pure polyester?

- that a single kumquat contains more roughage than hundredweight of bran?

- that Norwich is 200 feet higher above sea level than Mexico City?

- that each of the 50 stars on the US flag represents a different strain of herpes?

- that Ernest Hemingway was inspired to write *Death In The Afternoon* after a fruitless day's shopping for a shirt in Oxford Street?

- that the amount of rubber contained in the human body is enough to make 300 condoms?

- that King Arthur's dentures are believed to be buried in the grounds of Glastonbury Abbey?

- that George Bernard Shaw had such a prodigious memory that he could recall precisely what he had had for lunch on any given date? Hitler's memory was so good he could recite entire pages of the Koran at will.

George Frideric Handel (1685–1759): of his ninety-nine cantatas, sixty-eight were written while he was upside-down in a yoga position.

● that the Market Weighton Canal in Humberside was once an important trade route to the Far East?

● that baked beans are a powerful aphrodisiac?

● that Trotsky had a premonition of death only minutes before his assassination, commenting to a friend 'my ears are burning'?

● that craters are caused by collapsing air pockets?

● that thanks to a strange quirk in local boundary changes made in 1982, the native tongue of Wiltshire is Hebrew?

● that the Grand Canyon is the world's largest open-cast mine?

● that if the entire population of China were laid end to end they would be used to it by now?

Bryan Ferry's passion for whippet racing caused friction within his band, Roxy Music: Ferry's insistence upon taking his whippets on the road with him led to the band's split after their 1983 tour.

On this day in 1599 Oliver Cromwell was born, leader of the Parliamentary Army in the English Civil War, and Lord Protector of England after the execution of Charles I. Cromwell didn't always live up to his puritanical image: he spent the last five summers of his life holidaying in Benidorm, cavorting with wenches and sporting a healthy tan. It was here that he wrote the song 'Y-Viva España!'

● that the longest day is 9 February?

● that the year 'Dot' is believed to have been 14BC?

● that Chinese whodunit books are written so that the identity of the culprit is revealed on the very first page?

● that many of the early convicts sent to Tasmania were sent there for motoring offences?

● that the planet Neptune is completely hollow?

● that there is not a single homosexual in Australia?

● that the Suez Canal has 3,453 locks?

● that God created the Earth in a fortnight? The idea that he did it in a week arose from a mistake during translation.

● that the original *Top Of The Pops* theme tune was 'Coronation Scot'?

● that the Assyrians knew about the microchip as long ago as the third millennium BC?

● that Group Captain Peter Townsend was so fed up over his split with Princess Margaret that he went off and formed The Who?

● that the Aztecs were wiped out because they suffered from congenital deafness, and so could not hear Cortez coming?

● that the League of Nations set up after World War I had a two-up, two-down system?

● that 'Tiny' Rowland got his nickname because he takes a size 5 shoe?

IT'S A FACT!

THE VERY FIRST MORSE CODE MESSAGE SENT ACROSS THE ATLANTIC BY THE INVENTOR OF THE WIRELESS, GUGLIELMO MARCONI, WAS 'PEASE PUDDING'.

IT'S A FACT!

IF HITLER HAD NOT CHOSEN TO ADOPT HIS MOTHER'S MAIDEN NAME, HE WOULD HAVE BEEN ADOLF McPHERSON!

THE DAVY LAMP was first pioneered as a useful aid for pearl divers in the murky waters surrounding Madagascar. One of the immediate benefits gained by the new lamp was a drastic reduction in the death rate of caged canaries, which were traditionally employed by the primitive divers to sniff out pearls.

IN ROBERT LOUIS STEVENSON'S original draft of *Treasure Island*, Ben Gunn was very specific when asking for cheese. Stevenson had him requesting a small portion of gruyère.

KEVIN'S COMET is the fastest and most regular of all comets, circumnavigating the entire solar system in little more than three minutes. Unfortunately it moves so quickly that the human eye cannot detect it.

BEFORE A TRAINEE yogi can be accepted as a high priest he must prove himself by consuming 6 hundredweight of Himalayan balsam in one sitting.

CHELSEA are the only English Football League team to have been founded by Carmelite nuns, although Port Vale once fielded an entire team of Gilbertine Friars in their push for promotion from the Fourth Division in a game against Tranmere Rovers in 1973. Tranmere won 4-1.

November 5

On this day in 1805 the Frenchman Ferdinand de Lesseps, designer of the Suez Canal, was born. He originally intended the canal to run through Central Africa, linking the Atlantic with the Mediterranean, but ran out of cement and had to settle for a much shorter version linking the Mediterranean with the Red Sea. He became so depressed by his failure that he drowned himself during a day out at Selsey Bill.

Did you know that Sylvester Stallone does America's Speaking Clock?

Trivia Quiz No.10

1 How many Mecca bingo halls are there in Mecca?
   (a) Three?
   (b) Sixteen?
   (c) Fifty seven?
   (d) One hundred and thirty two?

2 Which member of The Supremes did important work on the Quantum Theory? Was it:
   (a) Florence Ballard?
   (b) Diana Ross?
   (c) Mary Wilson?
   (d) Cindy Birdsong?

3 Which nineteenth-century statesman was known as 'the Godfather of Skiffle'? Was it:
   (a) Prince Metternich?
   (b) Viscount Palmerston?
   (c) William Ewart Gladstone?
   (d) Benjamin 'Does Your Chewing Gum Lose Its Flavour on the Bedpost Overnight' Disraeli?

4 Who invented aspirin? Was it:
   (a) Dr Antoine Hedex?
   (b) Serge Anadin?
   (c) Sir Charles Paracetamol?
   (d) Dr Hugo Feminex?

5 Which English novelist wrote his entire body of work in Esperanto? Was it:
   (a) Charles Dickens?
   (b) Graham Greene?
   (c) D.H. Lawrence?
   (d) Samuel Richardson?

ANSWERS: 1 — (d); 2 — (c); 3 — (d); 4 — (d); 5 — (a).

IT'S A FACT!

BILL WYMAN IS THE OLDEST STONE BUT HE IS VERY COY ABOUT HIS REAL AGE. ACCORDING TO HIS PRESS AGENT HE IS 50: ACCORDING TO HIS MILITARY RECORDS HOWEVER HE WAS DISCHARGED FROM THE ARMY WITH VERRUCAS IN WORLD WAR I.

A POWDER ROOM (or ladies' lavatory) was originally so called because ladies once used to load their muskets with powder and shot in the course of attending to their toilet.

DORSET'S famous hill carving of a giant man near Cerne Abbey was covered up by the prudish Victorians, who commissioned a giant pair of underpants to be etched into the hillside. The underpants have since been removed.

On this day in 1870 the psychologist Alfred Adler was born. He believed that man's main driving force was the desire to play the harmonica.

DID YOU KNOW that Eve tempted Adam with a kumquat?

THE TINY South American tree frog — about the size of a human thumbnail — has an unquenchable thirst. In spite of the tree frog's diminutive stature it is capable of drinking more water than the largest of mammals: in 1953 a group of tree frogs on a binge slaked their thirsts by drinking dry the entire Amazon basin, thus causing untold damage to the region. Nature has a happy knack of keeping all things in balance, however: fortunately, the thirsty little tree frog is also the most incontinent of creatures and the whole problem was solved later that same evening!

In some of the more remote parts of Java, former Manchester City striker Franny Lee is still worshipped as a god.

Hess displays his boxer shorts — 'der
Grossmaxschmellinghosen' — to an
impressed Führer in 1939.

THE PART of a man's anatomy
which turns a woman on the most is·
the inside of his nostrils.

DURING THE SECOND World
War, when it was realised that there
were not enough barrage balloons
to deter German bombers, the
British resorted to filling walruses
with helium gas and floating them
above the capital.

DID YOU KNOW...?

- that Shakespeare wrote his best sonnets after eating kippers?

- that, pound for pound, the strongest creature in the animal kingdom is the polyp?

- that Princess Diana's wedding dress had 40,000 mulberry leaves sewn into the lining to make it rustle more?

- that King George III was so mad he once tried to bite off his own testicles?

- that Hereward the Wake wrote a treatise on Marsh Gas?

- that the major exports of Wales are sugarbeet and tinned peaches?

- that Paganini invented the tremolo arm?

- that the Arapahoe Indians invented the foxtrot?

- that Lady Godiva suffered from alopecia?

- that the four horsemen of the apocalypse are Conquest, Slaughter, Famine and Snooker?

- that fruit flies can live to be 200 years old?

- that an Indian elephant can hold 170 gallons of kaolin and morphine in its trunk?

- that if all of the atomic nuclei in the entire universe were squashed tightly together, you could keep them in your fridge for only a week before they went off?

Jenny Lind became the darling of US forces in Vietnam with her repertoire of anti-Communist songs: she was known as 'The Little Corncrake'.

December
20

On this day in 1813 one of the greatest western philosophers of modern times, Søren Aabye Kierkegaard, was born. He was an intensely miserable man who never went out unless it was to watch his favourite Scottish Football League team, St Mirren. It was on the terraces of St Mirren's ground that, after a string of particularly poor results, he founded the school of philosophy known as existentialism.

December 31

On this day in 1986 it was calculated that the novel *Moby Dick* had become the third highest selling book in the history of Western literature. It was based upon the real-life story of a mutant anchovy which had strayed perilously close to Windscale beach where it had consumed quantities of contaminated plankton.

KING HAROLD could not have been shot through the eye with an arrow at the Battle of Hastings. The Bayeaux Tapestry shows that he was wearing thick-lensed spectacles at the time. Also shown on the epic tapestry is Harold's primitive hearing aid.

THE ELGIN MARBLES are a bag of 'shotties' brought home from Greece by Lord 'Shotty' Elgin in 1812. The collection comprises eight 'ironies', five blue, red and green marbles and twenty or so smaller assorted coloured glassy marbles.

DID YOU KNOW that Bengalese tigers devour their prey by osmosis — a particularly slow and painful death for their victims?

STONEHENGE has been the subject of much fanciful speculation for centuries: one of the more bizarre theories put forward was that the stones were part of an early observatory used for astronomical and mathematical calculations! Scholars are now reasonably convinced, however, that Stonehenge was merely an ancient Druid gymnasium. The priests established a keen bodybuilding culture, believing that a good work-out was as important to the mind and body as their other rituals. Pumping stone therefore became part of the daily routine.

ETON is the only public school in England still practising fenestration as a daily form of corporal punishment for truants. Minor offences — such as failure to maintain a clean gym kit — are only punishable by *auto da fé*, a method popularised by the Portuguese Church for burning heretics.

IT'S A FACT!

KARL MARX WAS THROWN OUT OF THE BRITISH LIBRARY BECAUSE HE OWED RECORD FINES FOR NON-RETURN OF BOOKS!

Jack 'The Hat' McVitie: his murder led to a sensational thirty-nine-day trial in 1969 which put the Kray Twins behind bars for life.

_____

DID YOU KNOW that Bernard Matthews is a vegetarian?

* * * * * * * * * * * * *

THE AVERAGE North American 'grid-iron' football player is under 9 stone in weight and under 5 foot tall: the rest of their apparent bulk is padding and framework.

* * * * * * * * * * * * *

SIR EDMUND HILLARY'S successful assault upon Mount Everest in 1953 was his fourth attempt to conquer the world's most famous mountain and a testimony to the great man's perseverance and dogged British determination. Hillary's first two expeditions ended abruptly when he twice failed to negotiate the steps at New Cross station. He actually reached the Everest foothills on the third attempt in 1951, but the euphoria was short-lived: largely because of bad planning and even worse advice from the National Geographic Society, he insisted upon attempting to drive a team of fully grown huskies up Everest's treacherous South Col.

THE ROMAN EMPEROR Vespasian's life seemed to revolve around the letter 'V'. Apart from his name (and the fact that he was often victorious) he led the Vth Roman Legion, he could not count past V, he had a wife named Veronica and a girlfriend named Vanessa: his best friend was named Vic, he had verrucae on his feet, varicose veins in his legs and various types of VD!

DID YOU KNOW...?

● that former Leeds United centre-half Norman Hunter wrote *Tess of The D'Urbervilles*?

● that Hereward the Wake suffered from insomnia?

● that honey is extracted from the lymph glands of puff adders?

● that Sirius, the 'Dog Star', is so-called because it has an irregular shape similar to that of an English springer spaniel?

● that white people are white because they lack the development of the pigment chlorophyll, and should really be green?

● that to help pass the time on their great journey to Valhalla, Viking chieftains were always burned with their dart boards?

● that Stalin's first decree was effectively to ban the use of sunbeds in the Soviet Union?

● that Franz Klammer learned to ski via a correspondence course because his native Holland was too flat?

● that the old music-hall favourite 'Never Shut Your Mother In The Back Yard' was later altered and adopted as the famous Eton Boating Song?

● that outlaw Billy the Kid was an English aristocrat?

● that Russian discotheques only employ women bouncers?

● that Mae West's incredible libido was due to the fact that she suffered terribly from ingrowing toenails?

● that Samson lost all his strength because Delilah bit off his cold sore?

● that the Khyber Pass is situated between Conway and Llanfairfechan?

Mafia boss 'Lucky' Luciano. Did you know that he earned his nickname because he twice lost his brolly on the New York subway, but got it back from lost property both times?

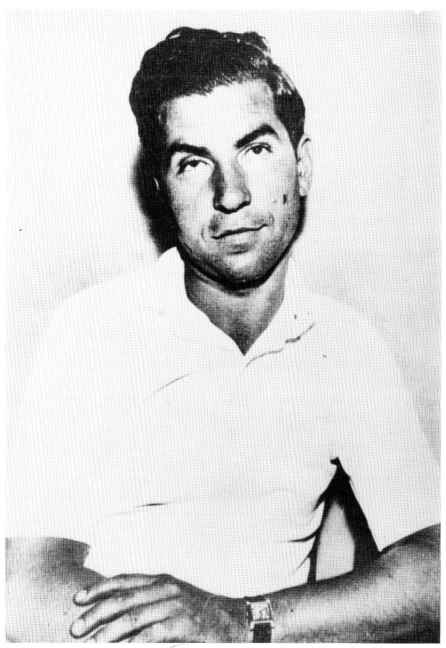

In parts of Switzerland the nearest tobacconist is sometimes hundreds of miles away: the Swiss have therefore evolved pipes capable of taking more tobacco, thus enabling a longer smoke.

* * * * * * * * * * * * * *

Did You Know...?

● that Michelangelo artexed the ceiling in Selfridges?

● that rock and roll began in Cheltenham?

- that the ancient Egyptians preserved mummies by coating them with jam?

- that the Rock of Gibraltar is inhabited by a colony of walking catfish?

- that the Queen's five corgis are named Mick, Keith, Bill, Ronnie and Charlie?

- that in New Zealand, surgical appliances were once used as hard currency?

- that Sir Geoffrey Howe was the original presenter of *The Old Grey Whistle Test*?

- that every Friday evening, members of the House of Lords compete for economy-size tins of Libby's peaches in a prize bingo session?

- that Bootle in Lancashire has more chiropodists per square mile than any other town in England?

- that Colonel Gadaffi is a keen fan of US 'Grid Iron' football? His favourites are the Washington Redskins.

- that a binary star is simply a star you have to look at twice before you can see it?

- that Nuneaton got its name from an obscure Order of arm-wrestling nuns?

- that the Tamar Bridge connecting Devon with Cornwall was built by Japanese prisoners-of-war?

- that Sigmund Freud had an irrational fear of cheese?

- that Chinese theologists believe in the existence of a Holy Wok?

- that between 1963 and 1966 Che Guevara was three times voted Argentinian Young Businessman Of The Year?

- that, thanks to a remarkable feat of engineering skill by James Brindley, the Grand Union Canal is also a jacuzzi?

ALTHOUGH THE QUEEN is probably the richest woman in the world, the Royals are well known for their thrift. Her Majesty's gift to Sarah Ferguson on the occasion of her marriage to Prince Andrew was a yoghurt-maker purchased from an Argos catalogue, and the Queen once had coin-operated loos installed throughout Balmoral. They had to be removed eventually because of the considerable inconvenience caused to the Duke of Edinburgh, who seldom carries money.

BRIAN, a hamster from Mousehole in Cornwall, holds a unique record for the compulsive swallowing of unusual objects. When Brian died in 1976 veterinary surgeons examined the contents of his stomach and found a 6-pound anchor, a fishing rod, a trawl net, a shark's head, a rabbit, a rowing boat, two cats, a mini-submarine, the remnants of a small lighthouse, several Richard Clayderman records and a one-legged cormorant.

Did You Know...?

● that the Great Plague started in a Derbyshire estate agent's and was spread by coypu?

● that it is said that a person can find out Elizabeth Taylor's age by counting the number of rings on her fingers?

● that, such was his professionalism and dedication to the role, throughout the filming of '*The Elephant Man*' actor John Hurt demanded a regular supply of buns?

● that two of the Beverley Sisters were All Blacks?

● that sheep sleep on their backs?

SELECT TRIVIOLOGRAPHY

Not Many People Know This About The Franco-Prussian War — A.P.J. Tailor
Not Many People Know This Either About The Franco-Prussian War — A.P.J. Tailor
A Trivial Guide to the Struggle For Mastery In Europe 1848–1918 — A.P.J. Tailor
1,000 Things You Never Knew About Bismarck — A.P.J. Tailor
From Napoleon To Stalin: Great European Leaders In Their Underpants — Paula Yates & A.P.J. Tailor
One Hundred Things You Thought You Knew About Communism — Karl Marx
Mein Kampf: The Ultimate Trivia Edition — A. Hitler
An Utterly Trivial Guide to World War I — Winston Churchill
Du Contrat Social (Baby Boomer Edition) — Jean-Jacques Rousseau
The Origin Of Species: It's A Fact! — Charles Darwin
Crime and Punishment: The Family Fun Trivia Quiz Game — F. Dostoevsky
Everything You Need To Know About Uncle Vanya But Didn't Dare To Ask — A. Chekhov
The Bizarre But True Economic Consequences Of The Peace — J.M. Keynes
Yet Another Thirty-Nine Steps! — J. Buchan
Unacceptable Facts of Capitalism — E. Heath
Trivial Hirsute — V. Sassoon